INSIGHT COMPACT GUIDE

Be

GW00367163

Compact Guide: Berlin is the ultimate quick-reference guide to the reunited German metropolis. It tells you all you need to know about Berlin's multitude of attractions, from the Brandenburg Gate to Unter den Linden, from the Pergamon Museum to Potsdam.

This is one of over 100 titles in Insight Guides' series of pocket-sized, easy-to-use guidebooks intended for the independent-minded traveller. *Compact Guides* are in essence travel encyclopedias in miniature, designed to be comprehensive yet portable, as well as up-to-date and authoritative.

Star Attractions

An instant reference to some of Berlin's most popular tourist attractions to help you on your way.

Brandenburg Gate p14

Zeughaus p19

Pergamon Altar p22

Zoo p30

Schloss Charlottenburg p44

Egyptian Museum p46

Hans Holbein p61

Skulpturenabteilung p62

Peacock Island p72

Schloss Sanssouci p77

BERLIN

Introduction

Places

Culture

Leisure

Practical Information

Berlin – A City Reunited

The historic decision on Germany's capital city has been made. Berlin never believed it would happen, but on 20 June 1991, after months of controversy, the Bundestag voted by a majority of 18 to move the parliament and the seat of government of a united Germany to the city on the Spree. All government buildings will be located in the old diplomatic quarter of the city, known as 'Mitte' or in the Tiergarten district, but the move from Bonn to Berlin will probably not be completed until the year 2002 because of all the construction work required.

To transform Berlin into Germany's seat of government is not the only challenge facing the reunited city. The tasks which now confront Berlin are of such huge proportions that Berliners who had become accustomed to an introspective existence in the shadow of the Wall, sometimes take fright at what is in store for them. This applies particularly to the inhabitants of the eastern part of the city, which has become a mass of construction sites. For many, the euphoria that followed the collapse of the Wall in 1989 has been replaced by a certain scepticism. Life no longer seems as secure as it once was. The Berlin Wall may have fallen, but it will take a long time before the wall inside people's heads has been dismantled.

Many hands make light work

5

Rearranging the Wall

City of culture

With all the city's transitional problems, expectations are high for Berlin's cultural role. As a capital city, there is huge potential. Ensuring that Berlin, as Germany's major artistic and cultural centre, can compete favourably with London, Paris and Rome has become an important concern. Berlin has no less than 150 established theatres, including the famous Schaubühne, which, until 1991, was under the artistic direction of Peter Stein, the legendary Deutsche Theater, once home to Max Reinhardt, and three opera houses. There are also some 200 independent theatres operating in the city. The Berlin Philharmonic, which has a new successor to Claudio Abbado in Sir Simon Rattle, is one of the finest orchestras in the world.

Berlin's museums contain countless treasures. After London and Paris, the city's museums are regarded as the most important in Europe. There are over a hundred museums in Berlin, some of which house collections of world-wide renown, but there are also some much humbler establishments such as the Dog Museum, the Teddy Bear Museum and the Sugar Museum.

Location and size

Berlin lies at the heart of Europe. It stands on the same line of longitude as Naples, 13.25E and on approximately the

Tranquillity at the Tegeler See

The slower pace of Pfaueninsel

same parallel as London, 52.31N. From the eastern tip of the city to the west is a distance of 45km (30 miles), and from north to south about 38km (22 miles). It is surrounded by the German Federal State (Land) of Brandenburg which lies on the rivers Spree and Havel.

In terms of area and population, Berlin is the biggest city in Germany. The German cities of Munich, Stuttgart and Frankfurt am Main could easily be accommodated within the confines of Greater Berlin. On average, it stands 35–60m (100–180ft) above sea level, covering an area of 883sq km (335sq miles). What used to be West Berlin represents 54.4 percent (480sq km/182sq miles) of the city, while 45.6 percent (403sq km/153sq miles) lies in the eastern sector. The built-up areas of west Berlin amount to slightly more than a third of the total area. In the eastern half, only about half of the area has been developed.

Rivers, lakes and woodland

Berlin is on the Spree and the Havel. The Spree rises in the Lusatia region in the southeastern corner of Germany and flows into the Grosser Müggelsee on the outskirts of the city. From here it flows into the central district where it splits to make Museum Island and eventually joins with the Havel in Spandau. The Tegeler See, the Müggelsee and the Wannsee are the most attractive lakes in Berlin, but there are 62 altogether, not to mention the 127 other waterways which include inlets, canals (and more bridges than Venice). No other German city has such a vast recreational area on its doorstep. On fine weekends city-dwellers flock to the Grunewaldsee, the Schlachtensee, Krumme Lanke, Havelchaussee, Heligensee and Rummelsburger See. Only a little further beyond, there are many deserted beauty spots. It is not true to say that there are only pine forests in Berlin. In the mixed woodland of the Spandau, Tegel and Düppel forests, walkers will stumble across marshland, bogs, tiny lakes and ponds.

Climate

Berlin lies in the transitional zone between maritime and continental weather patterns. The Berlin climate would be best described as 'relatively dry'. The average rainfall total of 600mm (25in) per year is appreciably below that of Munich and Bonn. The annual mean temperature is 9.3°C (49°F), which ranges from 0.7°C (33°F) in January to 19.1°C (67°F) in July.

Population

The people of Berlin come from far afield. There may be a lot of outsiders but even the newly arrived residents are never referred to as that. Wherever you come from, if you live in Berlin, you are a Berliner. Those special qualities can be 'learnt'. The city's first German settlers came mainly from the Lower Rhine area, but it was the east, Silesia, Pommerania and East Prussia where most Berliners originated from. 'A proper Berliner comes from Silesia' is a remark than can still be heard. At the end of the 17th century, 6,000 French Huguenots fled to Berlin and were quickly assimilated. Many surnames bear witness to this influx of French blood. Over the centuries, Berlin has withstood the arrival of so many settlers. Until recently they came from the west, but now the Wall has been dismantled, once again they are coming from the east.

Berlin has 3.4 million inhabitants (4.5 million in 1943) with 2.2 million living in the west and about 1.3 million in the east, but the actual number of inhabitants in the west is probably some 100,000 higher than the official figures. Many immigrants have settled in the poorer parts of the city, namely Wedding, Tempelhof, Neukölln and notably Kreuzberg or 'Little Istanbul' – the smallest district in area but the most densely populated. Thirty-two percent of Kreuzberg's population hails from other countries, predominantly Turkey.

A hopeful glance

The Berliner and his language

Goethe once described the Berliner as 'a daring breed of man' but to get closer to them 'you need to have hair on your teeth, and to keep yourself above water, be a bit thick-skinned too'. Goethe's words hint at what the locals call *die Berliner Schnauze* or the Berlin lip, a cheeky manner which loves to puncture the pride of the self-important and challenge hypocrisy with confidence and humour. But Berliners have undergone many difficult times, which they have faced with a remarkable composure, certain of their ability to weather the storm. The quick-witted Berliner with his cautious scepticism often comes across to strangers as brusque and unfriendly, but it pays to spend more time in his company as it will soon become apparent that behind the 'lip' there's a big heart.

A daring breed of man

The local economy

Despite decades of partition and all the difficulties which faced businesses and forced many large companies to relocate, Berlin is still the biggest industrial city in Germany, and the third largest industrial centre in Europe after London and Paris. Capital city status and the end of the Cold War promises an exciting future for the city as multi-national companies look towards expanding markets in the east. Electrotechnology is undoubtedly the most important industry, with major contributors such as Siemens, AEG, SEL and OSRAM now well established. Some companies with world-wide reputations have left their mark on the city by bestowing their names on residential estates:

Siemenstadt and Borsigwalde. Engineering, food production, chemicals, pharmaceuticals (Schering) and textiles are also important contributors to the local economy.

Apart from the manufacturing industries, a large number of Berliners are employed in the service industries. The impressive reputation of Berlin's universities has attracted scientists and researchers. Berlin is also Germany's biggest academic centre.

Heed the construction signs

Construction and housing

Major construction projects in the heart of the city include the government sector, the Reichstag, Friedrichstrasse and Potsdamer Platz. The latter is a massive development funded by Daimler and Sony, and work here began towards the end of 1993. It is not just the central district of Berlin that needs rebuilding; the city simply needs more living accommodation. Many western districts such as Neukölln, Wedding and Kreuzberg, which were on the fringes of the divided city and for whom the Wall was too close for comfort, now find themselves back at the heart of the city and that has already had a dramatic effect on the district's social structure.

Housing planners in Berlin face serious problems in the coming years. In the east, 600,000 flats need modernising and the city needs between 80,000 and 100,000 new homes. In some districts of Berlin (Kreuzberg, Schöneberg, Neukölln, Wedding, Prenzlauer Berg), much of the housing stock is still tenement blocks dating from the end of the last century. Guest workers, pensioners, students and drop-outs have moved into these flats in Kreuzberg or Prenzlauer Berg and created their own culture. Both districts enjoy a lively alternative nightlife, but one consequence of the Wall coming down has been a steep increase in rents which may in turn change the social make-up of these districts yet again.

Alternative culture in Prenzlauer Berg

In the eastern sector of the city, between 1949 and 1989, 334,500 new apartments were built. Marzahn, Hohenschönhausen and Hellersdorf have grown into satellite towns for many thousands of people, but the apartment blocks have all been built in the same drab 'panel' style seen throughout the former East Germany. Since 1961, the old city centre – Unter den Linden and the Gendarmenmarkt – has been rebuilt or restored. The Nikolaiviertel is one small area which was restored in the old Berlin style. The East German government's ministerial buildings were built around the Schlossplatz and the Palast der Republik (Palace of the Republic) and the buildings surrounding Alexanderplatz are typical examples of socialist architecture. New government buildings are planned for this area, as well as for Spreebogen and around Leipzigerstrasse. Work began in 1993 on a shopping arcade near

Friedrichstrasse, which has now become the major shopping street for the eastern side of the city. Leipzigerstrasse is destined for the same kind of development.

Berlin politics
The whole reunited city has been governed from the central district since September 1991, when the mayor and the senate moved out of the the town hall in Schöneberg to the Rotes Rathaus (Red Town Hall), an imposing red-brick building near Alexanderplatz.

The Red Town Hall

Berlin is no longer a city of four sectors: the Allied powers finally pulled out of the city in October 1994.

The Berlin boroughs
The boundaries of modern Berlin were largely established in 1920 under the so-called *Gebietsreform* (boundary reform). For mainly administrative reasons, the six districts of Wedding, Tiergarten, Kreuzberg, Mitte, Prenzlauer Berg and Friedrichshain were amalgamated with seven neighbouring towns, numerous independent municipalities and suburbs to make Greater Berlin. At the same time, the city was divided into 20 new administrative *Bezirke* (boroughs). After 1979, three new *Bezirke* were added to the eastern sector: Marzahn (1979), Hohenschönhausen (1985) and Hellersdorf (1986). Apart from Tiergarten, Zehlendorf, Mitte and Weissensee, each Bezirk has well over 100,000 inhabitants. Three *Bezirke* can regard themselves as medium-sized cities, with more than 200,000 inhabitants, namely Spandau, Reinickendorf and Neukölln.

9

Historical Highlights

Excavations have revealed that as long ago as 8000BC a settlement existed where the city of Berlin now stands. Suevian tribes lived here in 1000BC, but from AD200–300, the Teutonic Burgundi tribe settled in the region and stayed until around AD650 when Slavonic Wends occupied the area. In 928 Heinrich I conquered the town of Brandenburg and a 200-year struggle for supremacy between the Slavonic and the Germanic peoples began.

1134 The Ascanian Albrecht the Bear is replaced by Kaiser Lothar as the Markgraf (Margrave) of Nordmark. In 1150 he declares himself the Markgrave of Brandenburg.

About 1230 The Ascanian margraves Johann I and Otto III found the two settlements of Cölln and Berlin on the banks of the Spree, from which modern Berlin evolved.

1320 When the Ascanian dynasty dies out, the Mark (Marches) of Brandenburg, as it is now known, falls to the Wittelsbach dynasty. Rivalry grows between Cölln and Berlin, but they still become important centres for merchants.

1415 The Nuremberg Burggraf (Burgrave) Friedrich von Hohenzollern is granted the Mark of Brandenburg and the rank of Kurfürst (elector) by Kaiser Sigismund, becoming Frederick I.

1442–70 Kurfürst (Elector) Frederick II annuls the union between Berlin and Cölln agreed in 1432, builds a castle on the banks of the Spree and takes up residence in 1470.

1618–48 Berlin is drawn into the Thirty Years' War. The population, which was 12,000 in 1618, is halved by the end, mainly due to the plague.

1640–88 The Great Elector, Frederick William, sets about the task of rebuilding the now impoverished city. He invites foreign artists to Berlin, welcomes the French Huguenots, founds trading companies and small industries, fortifies Berlin and links the Oder and the Elbe with the Friedrich-Wilhelm canal. The villages of Friedrichswerder and Dorotheenstadt grow up outside the fortifications.

1688–1713 Elector Frederick III, who on his accession in 1701, becomes King Frederick I, continues his father's plans for Friedrichstadt. In 1710 Berlin has a population of 56,000.

1713–40 King Frederick William I, the 'soldier king', extends Friedrichstadt.

1740–86 King Friedrich II (Frederick the Great) gives Berlin the splendour of a European capital. During his reign, the population increases from 81,000 to 150,000. Around 1750, cotton and silk manufacturing gives Berlin a valuable industrial base, becoming the centre for textiles in Germany. In 1770, the Linden is rebuilt as a magnificent boulevard. In the Seven Years' War, Berlin is occupied by the Austrians and the Russians.

1786–97 King Frederick William II declares Berlin the 'City of the Enlightenment'.

1797–1840 Reign of King Frederick William III. After the military collapse of Prussia at the Battles of Jena and Auerstedt, Napoleon I marches on Berlin on 27 October 1806. Two years of French military occupation begins. In 1810, Wilhelm von Humboldt founds the prestigious Berlin University. In 1811, the father of gymnastics, F L Jahn, builds the first German gymnastics arena. With the defeat of Napoleon I, Berlin's revival begins. Schinkel, Rauch and Lenné set about building a new city. In 1838, a rail link opens between Berlin and Potsdam. In 1839, the first horse-drawn bus service comes into service between Alexanderplatz and Potsdamer Platz.

1840–61 Under King Frederick William IV, Berlin develops into one of the most important industrial centres in Europe. In 1848, the population stands at 400,000. On 18 March 1848, the March Revolution begins. Frederick William IV promises to help bring about the unification of Germany. A (short-lived) Prussian National Assembly is summoned. On 3 April 1849, Frederick William turns down the offer of the kaiser's crown.

1861–88 Reign of King William I (from 1871, Kaiser William I). Otto von Bismarck becomes the Prussian prime minister (1862–1890).

1867 With the defeat of the Austrians, Berlin becomes capital of the North German Federation and the seat of the Reichstag and Zollparlament. On

18 January 1871, the city becomes capital of the German Reich. The population reaches 826,000.

1888–1918 Kaiser William II reigns. He dismisses Prince Bismarck (20 March 1890). The city undergoes major social changes, and the population rises to 1.9 million. In 1902, the first section of underground railway is opened. On 9 November 1918, at the end of World War I (1914–18), the Reichstag proclaims the German Republic.

1920 Berlin and its suburbs become an urban municipality with a population of 1.4 million. During this period, known as the Weimar Republic, Berlin thrives as the political, economic and cultural centre of the German empire. But by 1932 unemployment in the city reaches 636,000.

31 January 1933 Hitler becomes chancellor, his stormtroopers marching through the Brandenburg Gate with massed flags and torches.

1936 The XI Olympiad is held in Berlin. Hitler uses the event for Nazi propaganda.

9–10 November 1938 Nazi stormtroopers take to the streets, vandalising and destroying Jewish synagogues, shops and other properties. The Kristallnacht (Night of Broken Glass) initiates a wave of persecution that reduces the Jewish population from 170,000 to a mere 5,000 by 1945.

1939–45 World War II. On 23 November 1943 prolonged air attacks on the German capital start and, on 21 April 1945, the Russians begin their land attack; Hitler commits suicide on 30 April and the Soviet Army overruns the city on 2 May. On 5 June, the four Allied Commanders assume control of Berlin and the city is divided into four sectors.

1946 On 20 October, representatives from the four main political parties (SPD, CDU, SED and LPD) are elected to the assembly, the only free election for the whole of Berlin for over 40 years.

1948 The Soviet Union withdraws from the Allied Control Council (20 March) and the Allied Command (16 June) and the blockade of Berlin begins. Supplies for the three western sectors have to be airlifted in each day. On 30 November, a new city council formalises the partition of the city.

1949 The blockade is lifted on 12 May. On October, the German Democratic Republic (GDR) is founded and Berlin becomes its capital.

1950 On 1 October West Berlin's new constitution comes into force. Ernst Reuter is elected mayor.

1953 On 17 June workers stage an uprising in East Berlin which is put down with armed force.

1957 In February, the Bundestag declares that Berlin is the capital of all Germany. On 3 October Willy Brandt becomes mayor.

13 August 1961 Work begins on the Wall. Railway links between East and West are cut.

1963 On 26 June American President John F Kennedy visits West Berlin and tells the people of Berlin: '*Ich bin ein Berliner*'.

1972 After the Berlin Agreement, West Berliners can visit East Berlin and travel in the GDR.

1981 Richard M Weizsäcker becomes mayor for the CDU, followed by Eberhard Diepgen in 1984.

1987–8 Berlin celebrates 750th anniversary and in 1988 is nominated European City of Culture.

1989 Berlin is governed by a coalition of SPD and 'Alternative' groupings headed by Mayor Walter Momper. On 9 November 1989, the Wall is opened. By mid-1990, parts of it have been dismantled.

1990 On 3 October, Berlin is formally reunified and elections on 2 December determine the representatives for the new council.

24 January 1991 Berlin council elects Eberhard Diepgen as the first mayor of a united Berlin since 1946. The ruling group is a coalition of the SPD and CDU. In September 1991, Berlin is once again governed from the Rotes Rathaus (The Red Town Hall). The federal parliament votes to move the seat of government to Berlin over 12 years.

1994 Russian, British and French forces withdraw from Berlin.

1999 Inauguration of the building of the Reichstag as the new German parliament, with the glass dome being designed by the British architect, Sir Norman Foster.

The Brandenburg Gate

Preceding Pages:
Poignant symbol of the past

Niche statue,
Brandenburg Gate

Route 1

★ Brandenburg Gate – ★ Unter den Linden –Berlin
Cathedral

The ★ **Brandenburg Gate** ❶ can be reached on foot
via Strasse des 17 Juni. In former times, only pedestrians, cyclists and taxis could go through the gate, but now
private vehicles are allowed pass through it.

The first gate, a fairly modest affair, was built on this
site in 1734 as one of 18 gates around the old city walls.
After the rise of Prussia to the status of a great power un-
der Frederick the Great, his successor Frederick William
II ordered that the splendid new boulevard Unter den Linden should have a worthy new structure at its end. Taking the gateway to the Acropolis in Athens as his example,
the master builder Carl Gotthard Langhans created the
Brandenburg Gate, his masterpiece, between 1788–91.
It is one of the most significant achievements of German
Classicism. The quadriga bearing Victoria is by Gottfried
Schadow. The large attic relief beneath the quadriga represents the triumphal procession of the goddess of victory,
the 32 metopes on the end walls show scenes from Greek
mythology, 20 flat reliefs on the walls of its passages de-
pict the life of Hercules and the statues standing in niches
in the north and south sides are of the goddess Athena and
the god Aries. The main structure is 65m (215ft) in width,
11m (35ft) deep and 26m (85ft) high. The central opening
is 6m (18ft) wide and the four openings to either side are
each 4m (12ft). In 1806, Napoleon carried the quadriga
to Paris as a trophy, but in 1814, after the wars of inde-

pendence, Marshall Blücher brought it back to Berlin. In the 19th and 20th century the Brandenburg Gate was the scene of great military parades and processions. It was a focus for the people in times of triumph and of potential revolution. In World War II the gate was badly damaged and the quadriga destroyed. The magistrate of east Berlin ordered repair work on the gate between 1956–8. The quadriga and Victoria were made to the original pattern and placed in their original position.

On 22 December 1989 the gate, which after the construction of the Wall in August 1961 had special symbolic significance, was reopened to pedestrians – a cause for great celebrations throughout the city.

Russian merchandise on Pariser Platz

All the buildings in **Pariser Platz**, which were laid out in the days of Frederick William I, were destroyed in World War II, including the French and American embassies, the Adlon Hotel and the house of the painter Max Liebermann who, after witnessing the torchlight parade by the Nazis on 30 January 1933, had the windows of his studio overlooking Unter den Linden blacked out. Now the square is being restored to its original splendour and the heirs of Liebermann have given Berlin architect Josef Paul Kleihues the task of rebuilding the Liebermann house.

The splendid boulevard ★ **Unter den Linden** gets its name from the four rows of linden trees planted along it. It is 1.4km (1,500yd) long and 60m (200ft) wide, and runs

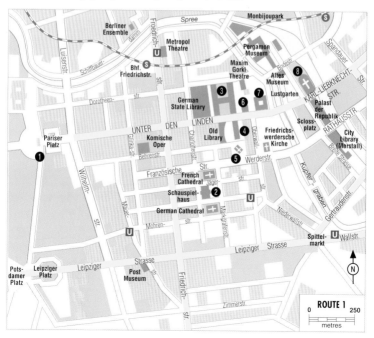

from the Brandenburg Gate to Schlossplatz. It was planned in the mid-17th century by the Great Elector and realised in its present form under Frederick the Great. It was damaged during World War II, but the historic buildings of the **Linden Forum** were rebuilt in the 1970s and its western end saw new building work. On the once famous junction with Friedrichstrasse only the Haus der Schweiz remains.

Instead of taking the direct route from the Brandenburg Gate via Unter den Linden to the Cathedral, it is possible to make a detour. The alternative route passes through the former government area, via Gendarmenmarkt and back to Unter den Linden. This area, the Whitehall of Berlin, was laid out by the first king of the Prussians, Friedrich I, and was called Friedrichstadt. It is defined by the two main roads forming the city's axes, Leipziger Strasse and Friedrichstrasse, but this part of the inner city suffered heavy damage during World War II.

Just behind the Brandenburg Gate turn right into Wihelmstrasse. Its face has been heavily marked by the course of politics. Until World War II this was where the British Embassy was situated, as was the Reichspräsidentenpalais (Palace of the President of the Reich), and the Foreign Office, the Reichskanzlei (Chancellery) as well as many other ministries. On Leipziger Strasse, which was once one of the busiest shopping streets in Berlin, there remains the Air Ministry built by Ernst Sagebiel between 1934–6. Turn left into Leipziger Strasse and the **Postmuseum** is situated at the corner of Mauerstrasse. It is housed in the Post Ministry, built between 1893–5.

Turn left into Friedrichstrasse and then right into Mohrenstrasse to reach the **Gendarmenmarkt ❷**. This

Strolling and cycling in Unter den Linden

The Schauspielhaus on Gendarmenmarkt

square takes its name from the *Gens d'armes* regiment which was housed there, together with their horses, between 1736–82. In 1950 its name was changed to Platz der Akademie, but in 1991 it reverted to its old name.

On the west side of the square is the ★ **Schauspielhaus**, built in 1819 and one of Schinkel's most beautiful buildings. He built it on the foundations of the National Theatre (1802, by Langhans the Elder) which was burnt down in 1817, but he managed to retain the Ionic columns of the portico. The reconstruction of the building, which had been largely destroyed during the war, was finished in 1984 with the facade faithfully restored and it was opened as a concert hall the following year. In 1988 Begas' **Schillerdenkmal** (Schiller memorial) dating from 1868 was restored.

Schiller memorial: detail

To the south of the Schauspielhaus stands the **Deutsche Dom** (German cathedral) and to the north the **Franzö-sische Dom** (French cathedral), both of which were built shortly after 1700 and to which Gontard added the domed towers between 1750–85. The Französische Dom was built for the French community of Huguenot families which settled in Berlin from 1685 onwards having fled from religious persecution in France. The community still worships here today. The small **Huguenottenmuseum** with its Fontane documents tells the story of the Huguenots in France, Berlin and Brandenburg. The restoration of this building was completed in 1987. The restored Deutsche Dom accommodates the political exposition 'Questions to German history', which explains the development of German parliamentarianism.

The French Cathedral

Friedrichstrasse, a busy shopping street once again, leads south to Leipziger Strasse and north to Friedrichstrasse station, where one of Berlin's many antiques markets is held. The **Komische Oper** stands in Behrenstrasse which runs parallel to Unter den Linden and within a few minutes walk are two theatres, the Berliner Ensemble, founded by Brecht, and the Deutsche Theater in Schumannstrasse, as well as the Friedrichstadt palais, and the Distel cabaret.

Back on Unter den Linden, continue towards Schlossplatz as far as Unter den Linden 13–15, where the exhibition hall **Deutsche Guggenheim Berlin** shows fine, changing art collections. Nearby is the **Staatsbibliothek zu Berlin** (the State Library for Prussian Cultural Heritage) in the neo-baroque building on the left-hand side of the street, which was the former Prussian State Library. Adjacent is the **Humboldt University ❸**. The main building was erected between 1748–66 by Johann Boumann as a palace for Prince Heinrich, the brother of Frederick II. In 1810, on the initiative of the eminent philologist Wilhelm von Humboldt, the building was converted to a seat of learning. Its first rector was Johann Gottlieb Fichte

Humboldt University

(1762–1814). Among the other renowned academics to work here were the philosophers Hegel and Schleiermacher, philologists Jacob and Wilhelm Grimm, physicists Helmholtz, Max Planck, Albert Einstein, Otto Hahn, physicians Virchow, Koch, Sauerbruch, and many others.

Also part of the university buildings are the former governor's house (Unter den Linden 11) and the Altes Palais (Unter den Linden 9). The site of the governor's house used to be occupied by the Dutch Palace which was damaged in World War II. The governor's house (1721) originally stood on the corner of Rathausstrasse and Jüdenstrasse but had to move to make way for new buildings during the reconstruction of the city centre (1967). Its baroque facade was carefully dismantled and used to fill a gap left by a war ruin. In front of the university, in the middle of Unter den Linden, stands the equestrian statue of Frederick II by the sculptor Christian Daniel Rauch (1851).

Opposite the university is **Bebelplatz**. This was planned by Frederick the Great as the Forum Fridericianum. The opera house, the Old Library and Cathedral of St Hedwig combine to create a masterpiece of urban architecture.

The Opera House

The **Deutsche Staatsoper (German State Opera House) ❹** was built as a royal opera house for Frederick the Great between 1741–3 by Georg Wenzeslaus von Knobelsdorff. After suffering serious fire damage in 1843 which left only the main walls standing, it was rebuilt in the same style. In World War II it was completely destroyed, but after historically faithful reconstruction work between 1952–5, during which only the auditorium (1,452 seats) was altered, it was reopened. Further restoration work was undertaken in 1986.

St Hedwig's Cathedral

Just behind the opera house stands **St Hedwig's Cathedral ❺**. The cathedral was begun on Frederick the Great's orders in 1747, according to designs by Jean Legeay and was completed by Boumann in 1773. The Pantheon in Rome served as its model. In World War II it was seriously damaged but was rebuilt between 1952–63. Today it is the cathedral church of the Catholic Bishop of Berlin.

Built in high Austrian baroque style by von Boumann between 1775–80, the **Alte Königliche Bibliothek** (Old Library), popularly known as *Die Kommode* (dressing table), stands on the west side of Bebelplatz. Severely damaged in World War II, it was rebuilt in the late 1960s.

Alte Königliche Bibliothek

To the left of the opera house is the former Prinzessinnenpalais, which was built in 1732, and is now called the **Opernpalais**. This too has been rebuilt and now houses two restaurants and a fine, Viennese-style café . On the lawns between the Operncafé and the opera house, ★ **statues** of the military leaders of the Wars of Independence were erected in 1962. These figures of Blücher, Yorck, Gneisenau and Scharnhorst are by Rauch. Through an arch connected to the Opernpalais is the former **Kronprinzen-palais** (Crown Prince's Palace), built in 1734, reconstructed between 1968 and 1969 and now looking again as it did originally. It was here that the Treaty of Unification between the two German states was signed on 31 August 1990.

Built by Karl Friedrich Schinkel between 1816–8 in the style of a Roman fort, the ★ **Neue Wache** ❻ was once the headquarters for the King's Guard. In 1960, it became the Memorial to the Victims of Fascism and Militarism. The interior, designed by Heinrich Tessenow between 1930–1, is a model of elegant simplicity. In November 1993, the building was inaugurated as the Central Memorial of the Federal Republic of Germany.

The Neue Wache

Behind the Neue Wache is the classical Singakademie, built in 1827 on the initiative of Carl Friedrich Zelters (1758–1832), a friend of Goethe. Today it is home to the Maxim Gorki Theatre.

Berlin's largest baroque building, and one of Germany's finest, is the ★ **Zeughaus (Armoury)** ❼. It was built between 1695–1706 according to plans by Nering von Grünberg, Schlüter and Jean de Bodt. Schlüter was also mainly responsible for the impressive ★★ **22 Warriors' Death Masks** in the courtyard known as the Schlüter-hof. This is another of those buildings badly damaged in World War II which received historically accurate treatment during its reconstruction. From 1952, it was the Museum of German History but it was closed in September 1990 because of its Marxist interpretation of events. Its future is now secure as plans are going ahead for it to house the Deutsches Historisches Museum (German Historical Museum), although due to renovation the house is actually closed again and will reopen in early 2002.

The Zeughaus

19

Death mask of a warrior

Opposite the Zeughaus, the memorial to the Imperial Baron vom und zum Stein has been re-erected. On Werderscher Markt is the neo-Gothic brick **Friedrichswerdersche Kirche**, built by Schinkel between 1824–8. In 1987 it was opened as the **Schinkelmuseum**, and shows a lot of marble sculptures from Berlin's classical period between 1780 and 1860. Another of Schinkel's creations, this time dating from 1822 and restored between 1982–4, is the **Schlossbrücke** (Palace Bridge) with historic figures by Schinkel, spanning the Kupfergraben, one of the arms of the Spree.

The bridge leads to the vast, treeless **Schlossplatz**. The square was originally part of the pleasure garden (or going even further back to 1573, the vegetable garden) in the grounds of the Berlin Stadtschloss, which was demolished in 1951. The palace had been the residence of the Hohenzollerns from 1451 to 1918 and at the time its demolition sparked vehement protests in both east and west. The palace had been one of Germany's most important baroque monuments. Schlüter worked on it between 1698–1706, as did Eosander von Göthe until 1713. Its Eosander portal was incorporated into the facade of the **State Council building**, which was constructed between 1962–4 and was relieved of its function in 1989. This building stands on the corner of Breite Strasse and since 1999 has housed the Bundeskanzlesamt (Federal Chancellery).

To the left, on the corner of Breite Strasse, is the former Royal Mews and to the right of the old State Council building, on Werderscher Markt, is the former East German Communist Party Central Committee building, the future of which is still being discussed.

The Friedrichswerdersche Kirche

The **Palast der Republik** (Palace of the Republic), which has recently been renamed the House of Parliamentarians, was opened in 1976 on the site of the demolished Stadtschloss. This unpopular building, which is known locally as *Palazzo Prozzo* (The Show-offs Palace), was closed even before the demise of the GDR regime because of asbestos contamination and it now stands empty. There are plans to put up government buildings and possibly a congress centre on and around the square. The part of the green square in front of the cathedral is known as the Lustgarten.

Berlin Cathedral

Berlin Cathedral ❽ was built by Julius Raschdorff in the style of the Italian High Renaissance between 1894–1905. The restoration of the exterior of the war-damaged church was completed in 1984. The restored Imperial Staircase was opened on 30 June 1989.

Beneath the church is the Hohenzollern crypt which is currently being renovated. The Great Elector, Frederick William, his wife Dorothea and Frederick William II are buried here.

Route 2

Colourful silks at the flea market on Museum Island

The ★★ Museumsinsel (Museum Island)

The state museums in Berlin comprise the Museum Island, the museum complex in Dahlem (*see pages 60–3*) and the Kulturforum at Kemperplatz (*see pages 42 and 43*), where the Painting gallery has just been completed. Despite the separation of Berlin's art treasures as a result of the division of the city, the ★★ **Museumsinsel** and its collections must rank as one of the world's finest museum complexes. This cluster of museums came about as the result of a decree by Frederick William III to the effect that the private art collections of the royal court were to be made accessible to the public. A new museum was to be built for that purpose, as had already happened in London and was about to happen in Paris.

The first museum to be opened was the Altes Museum, designed by Schinkel in 1830, and it was one of his most splendid creations. After the Glyptothek in Munich, it is the oldest museum building in Germany. But it soon proved to be too small, so between 1843–59 the Neues Museum was built directly behind it, according to Stüler's designs. This building, which was destroyed, is currently undergoing a faithful reconstruction and is due to house the Egyptian Museum. The Alte Nationalgalerie came into existence in 1876, and 1904 saw the opening of what is now the Bode Museum built by Ernst von Ihne between 1897–1903. The last museum to be finished was the Pergamon Museum, which had been started in 1909 but its completion was delayed during the war years and it was finally opened in 1930.

Altes Museum: Rotunda with sculptures

The ★ **Altes Museum (Old Museum)**, which was reconstructed following substantial damage in World War II and reopened in 1966, houses on the first floor the reunited Greek and Roman works of art from the former Antiken Museum in the west district of Charlottenburg, and the sculptures and small works from the Pergamon Museum. The circular rotunda, for which the Roman Pantheon served as a model, forms a splendid prelude to the main museum. The second floor is now due to feature changing exhibitions.

The ★ **Alte Nationalgalerie (Old National Gallery)** was built between 1867–76 by Strack, following Stüler's designs, in the form of a Corinthian temple. On the ornamental staircase is a memorial to Frederick William IV by Calandrelli (1886). During the Nazi period, 400 works were lost in the crusade against so-called 'degenerate' art. In addition, the Nationalgalerie suffered serious wartime losses.

Alte Nationalgalerie: Viktoria by Rauch

Be that as it may, the development of German art from the end of the 18th century to the early twentieth century is well-documented, from the time of Goethe to Expressionism. Although the National Gallery is closed for several years due to extensive renovation, when it reopens around 2002 it will display many works by Berlin artists, such as Krüger, Blechen, Menzel (including his famous ★ *Eisenwalzwerk* or Steel-rolling Mill), Liebermann, Ury, and also paintings by Slevogt and Corinth, masterpieces by ★ Caspar David Friedrich and ★ Böcklin's celebrated *Island of the Dead*.

The German Expressionists are represented by Kirchner, Pechstein, Nolde, Rohlfs and others, with sculptures by Barlach and Lehmbruck as well as 19th-century sculptures by Schadow *(Group of Princesses, Goethe)*, Canova, Rauch and Begas. French Expressionists are also represented. The Nationalgalerie owns the famous *Maypole* by the Spanish court painter ★ Francisco de Goya (1736–1828). Work from the 20th century includes the Bauhaus school, the *Brücke* movement, *Blauer Reiter* and photomontages by John Heartfield.

★★★ *The Pergamon Museum*

The Pergamon Museum is arguably the best-known museum on the Museum Island. This large building consisting of three wings was built between 1909 and 1930 to designs by Alfred Messels (1853–1909). It contains the ★★ Collection of Antiquities with the world famous ★★★ Pergamon Altar, the ★★ Near East Museum and the Islamic Museum.

The ★★ **Vorderasiatische Museum (Near East Museum)** provides a comprehensive overview of 4,000 years of Middle Eastern history, art and culture. The wealth of

Discover the Pergamon Museum

its treasures is exceeded only by that of the British Museum in London. Only a few exhibits come from fine art trade, most of them being discovered by archaelogical excavations, especially by German research teams between 1885 and 1939 in Asia Minor, South Anatolia, Turkish Armenia, Iraq, Syria and Iran.

The museum is particularly renowned for its architectural monuments, the most well-known of which is perhaps the ★★★ *Processional Way* and Nebuchadnezzar II's ★★ *Ishtar Gate* (604–562BC) in rooms 8 and 9. Shortage of space prevented the two structures from being restored to their actual size. The road is therefore only 8.5m (25ft) wide, whereas it was actually 60m (200ft) wide. Each side of the road depicts numerous yellow lions in relief on a blue background.

Ishtar Gate: detail

Opposite the Ishtar Gate is the great ★ *Facade of the Throne Room* (1st century BC). Also unique are the *Castle Gate of Sendschirli* flanked by four lions (10th–8th century BC), the *Victory Stele of the Assyrian King Asarhaddon* (680–669BC), the bas-reliefs and the *Great Bird of Tell Halaf* (c 900BC).

The ★★ **Antikensammlung (Collection of Antiquities)** the history and progress of the collection can be traced back to the time of the Great Elector. The collection gained in importance as a result of the acquisitions of Frederick the Great, including the purchase of Cardinal Polignac's collection from Paris in 1742 and the famous *Praying Boy* (4th century BC).

23

The Pergamon Altar

Arguably the most celebrated piece of the collection is, however, the ★★★ **Pergamon Altar** (180–160BC), a true masterpiece of Hellenistic architecture and sculpture, situated in the central hall. The altar describes the battle of the Gods against the Titans. Parts of the 120-m (350-ft) long frieze are installed on the west side of the altar and the remaining frieze is displayed on the walls. The altar steps lead to the adjoining room with the *Small Pergamon Frieze*, or the *Telephos Frieze*.

In the middle of the room there is the floor mosaic from the Palace of Attalos II (160–150BC). The altar was employed by the Attalide rulers for votive offerings. In 1886, the huge marble monument was uncovered after several archaeological digs on the west coast of Asia Minor. Another highlight of the collection is the monumental ★★ Market Gate from Miletus (c AD165) which is situated across two floors and dates from the time of Emperor Marcus Aurelius.

The Market Gate from Miletus

Among the truly wonderful works of early Hellenic sculpture on display, mention should be made of the ★ *Goddess with Pomegranate* (c AD575), the so-called Berlin Goddess, remarkable for its well-preserved polychrome coloration, the ★ *Enthroned Goddess from Tar-*

From the Islamic Museum

The majestic exterior of the Bode Museum

Stairs in the Bode Museum

ent (c 470BC) and the famous bronze statue of the ★ *Praying Boy* (4th century BC) – all of which are works of international importance.

The **Islamische Museum (Islamic Museum)**: Wilhelm von Bode, the celebrated German museum curator, is responsible for the foundation of the Islamic department in 1904. The collection gives a highly comprehensive overview of Islamic art from its earliest days right up to the present. Pride of place in the collection is taken by the ★ *Monumental Facade of the Desert Palace Mshatta* (c AD740), a gift from the Turkish sultan Abdulhamit to Kaiser William II.

The Aleppo Room (1600–3) has been faithfully reconstructed in the style of a Christian merchant. Other features that are equally well worth seeing include the extensive collection of Persian and Indian miniatures (14th–18th century) and the sculptures of the pre-Islamic dynasty of the Sassanites. These sculptures were excavated from Ktesiphon.

★ Bode Museum

This museum is surrounded by the River Spree at the northern tip of Museum Island and has a special atmosphere all of its own. It originally opened in 1904 as Kaiser-Friedrich Museum, but in 1958 its name was changed to that of its founder, Wilhelm von Bode (1845–1929), who had become well-known both at home and abroad as the long-standing chief curator of the Berlin museums and who had also helped them to acquire an impressive worldwide reputation.

The museum has to be completely restored and is therefor closed until the year 2001. In the future, the magnificent rooms will house the Museum for Late Antiquity and Byzantine Art, the Sculpture Collection, the Museum of

Islamic Art and the Coin Cabinet. The entrance hall shows the monumental equestrian statue of the Great Elector, Frederick William, as he founded what today is the collection of state museums in Berlin. A surprising impression is made by the Kamecke Hall, a built-in basilica, which is based on a model of the church San Salvatore al Monte in Florence.

The **Museum für Spätantike und Byzantinische Kunst (The Museum for Late Antiquity and Byzantine Art)** houses works of art from the Mediterranean dating from the 3rd to the 18th century. The artistic efforts of the Christian Egyptians (the Copts) are particularly well represented, but the ★ *Apsis Mosaic from the Church of San Michele in Africisco in Ravenna* (545) is the centrepiece of this early Byzantine (3rd–9th century) collection and certainly worth a visit.

A priceless expression

The **Sculpture Gallery** in the Bode Museum houses an extensive number of German, Italian, French, Spanish and Dutch works from early Christian icons to Italian sculptures from the Rococo period of the late 18th century. The Bode Museum is especially well known for its high rooms which make it possible to display large works, such as altar pieces, and choir stalls, to their best advantage. The German sculpture section emphasises works from the 15th and 16th century and includes such treasures as ★ Riemenschneider's *Naumburger Kruzifix*, the ★ *Trier Prophets*, and the ★ *Minden Altar*.

Madonna with Child in the Sculpture and Art Gallery

25

The **Münzkabinett (Coin Collection)** is one of the finest collections in the world with around half a million coins, medals, notes and seals. Its historical roots go back to the time of the Renaissance. Exhibits range about a thousand years, from the beginning of coining die in Classical Greek times during the sixth century before Christ, to the present day. Furthermore, the Coin Collection and its extensive special library serve as an international research institute.

The exhibition at the **Museum für Islamische Kunst (Museum of Islamic Art)** focuses on the significant role of Arabic script in the religion of Islam. In addition, there are displays of architectural features, such as the prayer niche with two friezes bearing script (Iran, 16th century) which give a clear impression of Islamic architecture. There are also stelae, carpets and secular and religious textiles on display.

Coin Collection exhibits

The **Kunstgewerbe Museum (Art and Craft Museum)** section of the Bode Museum is to be found in Schloss Köpenick (*see page 75*) and it exhibits European crafts from the late Middle Ages to the present day. The furniture collection is particularly extensive. Of special interest are the precious Gisela Jewels dating from AD1000 and the stunning Berlin silver service of King Frederick I.

Route 3

Old Town – Alexanderplatz – Karl-Marx-Allee

Baroque epitaph in the Marienkirche

This route passes through the oldest parts of the city, which were founded in the 13th century – Cölln (on the northern half of the present-day Museum Island) and Berlin (on the other side of the Spree by the town hall and Molkenmarkt). The two towns were connected by the Mühlendammbrücke, with the fish market in Cölln at one end of the bridge and the dairy market in Berlin at the other end. St Petri Church was founded near the market in Cölln and St Nikolas Church (Nikolaikirche) near the market in Berlin. Littenstrasse runs along the eastern part of the old Berlin town wall.

This sector of the city suffered substantial damage in World War II and had to be rebuilt. Only a few buildings here still give an impression of the old Berlin. From Berlin Cathedral (*see page 20*) walk down Karl-Liebknecht-strasse, which – like the pedestrian precinct of Rathaus-strasse that runs parallel to it – has been substantially broadened and built up with residential accommodation in the socialist architectural style.

Continue on to the **Marienkirche** ❾ (Monday–Saturday, 10am–4pm; Sunday 10am–6pm), the second oldest church in Berlin after the Nikolaikirche. Built at the beginning of the 15th century on the brick remains of a 13th-century building, the Gothic-style spire takes its present form

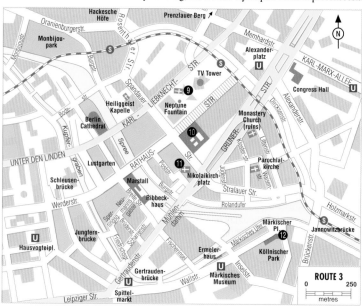

ROUTE 3

0   250

metres

from a design by Langhans in 1790. The *Cross of Atonement* in front of the church gate was built to commemorate the murder of the Provost of Bernau. The Luther Memorial was restored in 1989.

Inside the church is a baroque pulpit by Andreas Schlüter (1703), which was moved to face the choir when the church was restored after the war. In the hall of the belfry there is a 22-m (70-ft) medieval fresco called *Der Totentanz* (The Dance of Death), painted by an unknown artist and thought to have been inspired by an outbreak of the Black Death in 1484. The bronze font in the choir dates from 1437.

Inbetween Karl-Liebknechtstrasse and Burgstrasse behind the Plaza Hotel is the **Heiliggeistkapelle**, first mentioned in 1272 as a part of the hospital. The building, which is directly adjacent to the chapel, is used by the Humboldt University.

The Fernsehturm (television tower; *see page 30*) rises up from behind the Marienkirche. To the south of the church is the **Neptune Fountain** (1891) by Begas, which formerly graced the Schlossplatz. The bronze figures at its edge symbolise the four German rivers of the Rhine, the Weichsel, the Elbe and the Oder. Berliners say that the bronze women are 'the only women in Berlin who know when they should keep their mouths shut'.

On the other side of Rathausstrasse stands the **Rotes Rathaus (Town Hall) ❿**. Berlin's old town hall occupied this site as early as the late 13th century. The red brick building which stands here today – known to Berliners as the 'Red Town Hall' but not on account of its red facade – was constructed in neo-Renaissance style between 1861 and 1869 by H F Waesemann. Its square tower, 74m (225ft) high, soon came to be regarded as a landmark for Berlin. Curiously, the first sitting of the magistrates took place there in 1865, before it was completed. A frieze called

Red Town Hall: facade and window detail

27

the *Chronical of Berlin* encircles the first floor. In 1945, the Rathaus suffered severe damage and was rebuilt in 1955. In 1991, it became Berlin's seat of government again.

South of the Rathaus is the Molkenmarkt, the central square of old Berlin. In the middle stands the restored **Nikolaikirche** ⓫ from which the square takes its new name, Nikolaikirchplatz. Built around 1230, the Nikolaikirche is the oldest church in Berlin. This triple-naved building survived from 1470 until 1944 when it was bombed. Near the church, a part of old Berlin has been recreated: medieval dwellings known as a *Kiez* – a Slavonic word meaning a 'hut' – the famous Zum Nussbaum inn, and the **Ephraim-Palais**, which was constructed between 1761–5 for the banker and court jeweller of Frederick the Great. The original sandstone facade has been fully restored and it is now a gallery for exhibitions from the Märkisches Museum.

Towers of the Nikolaikirche seen from the banks of the Spree

Götthold Ephraim Lessing lived at Königsgraben 10 from 1765 until 1766 and completed his comedy, *Minna von Barnhelm* here. A plaque on the Nikolaikirchplatz indicates where the house stood. At the corner of Poststrasse (No 23) stands the classical-style **Knoblauchhaus**, an exhibition house, dating from 1765, which once belonged to the silk manufacturer Knoblauch and now belongs to the Märkisches Museum. It contains a permanent exhibition about the Knoblauch family. In the basement there are the Historic Wine Rooms and on the banks of the Spree nearby stands the statue *St George on Horseback* (1849).

The Knoblauchhaus

To the right, in the direction of the Spree, stands the former Ministry of Culture just to the left of Mühlendammbrücke. It comprises both the former building of the Reichsmünze (imperial mint) built between 1935–9 and the former Palais Schwerin (designed by Jean de Bodt in 1714). The facade displays the relief frieze by Schadow (1798) that was formerly a part of the old mint.

After crossing Mühlendammbrücke look for the fish market of Cölln and from there **Breite Strasse**, the largest and grandest street of old Berlin. Only a few of its beautiful houses have survived. The **Ermelerhaus** (1761), for example, was torn down and rebuilt on the Märkisches Ufer. It is now a restaurant. No 35 is the **Ribbeckhaus** (1624), the only Renaissance town house remaining in Berlin. It was built for the Ribbeck family – an aristocratic family from Brandenburg made famous in the poem by Theodor Fontane *Herr von Ribbeck on Ribbeck in Havelland*. Next to the Ribbeckhaus is the **Alte Marstall** (Old Mews) built between 1665 and 1670.

The Ribbeckhaus

Two houses are of interest in nearby Brüderstrasse. These also were once the homes of rich Berlin families – the Nicolaihaus and Galgenhaus (Gallows House). The **Nicolaihaus** at No 13, which was built in 1710, was the

home of the publisher and writer Friedrich Nicolai
(1787–1811). It soon became the literary meeting place
for Berlin. Visitors included the writer Anna Luise Karsch,
the illustrator Chodowiecki, Theodor Körner, Schadow,
Schinkel and the composer Carl Friedrich Zelter. Plaques
recall some of the house's famous guests. The **Galgenhaus** was built in 1680. An innocent servant girl is said
to have been hanged in front of it for appearing to have
stolen a silver spoon from the house's owner.

Jungfernbrücke (1798), close to Brüderstrasse, is the
last of nine drawbridges over the Kupfergraben.

The **Märkisches Museum** ⓬ is situated at Köllnischer
Park 5. For opening times *see page 83*. Take the S-Bahn
or U-Bahn to Jannowitzbrücke station or the U-Bahn to
Märkisches Museum station. The museum, which was
founded in 1874, was moved in 1908 to this substantial
castle-like brick building by the influential Berlin architect Ludwig Hoffmann. It houses permanent exhibitions
from the early and pre-historic greater Berlin area, and
portrays the development of the town from 1648 to 1815.
One section gives a fascinating insight into the history
of Berlin theatre from 1740 to the present day. Also on display are collections of Berlin glass, faience pottery and
porcelain, as well as Berlin painting, crafts and a collection of mechanical and musical instruments from the
baroque period to the present day.

Other artefacts belonging to the museum are to be found
in the Nikolaikirche, the Ephraim-Palais and the
Knoblauchhaus. Behind the museum is the small **Köllnischer Park** which contains a preserved section of the
city wall with a part of a tower (1658), the bear-pit and
a monument to Zille by H Drake.

The **Otto-Nagel-Haus** was established at the Märkisches
Ufer 16 in two old Berlin houses dating from the 17th and
18th century. In former times, it contained paintings, wa-
tercolours and drawings by this Berlin painter who was
closely allied with the working classes. Today it is the residence of the photo archives from the Preussischer Kulturbesitz, the organisation that manages Berlin's state
museums. At Märkisches Ufer 14 stands a town house from
the end of the 18th century. No 12 is in fact a copy of a rococo house in Friedrichsgracht. No 10 is the **Ermelerhaus**
which was moved here from Breite Strasse. It is the last
remaining house from the rococo period in Berlin, named
after its former owner, the tobacco merchant Ermeler.

*Otto-Nagel-Haus
with exhibit*

From the Märkisches Museum take the U-Bahn to Alexanderplatz and then to **Karl-Marx-Allee**. Walkers may
prefer to make a detour across the Spree via the Janowitz-
brücke behind the museum. Then turn left along Rolandufer
and cross diagonally to the right into Waisenstrasse. Here on
the edge of old Berlin, some remains of the city wall from

The World Time Clock

the 13th and 14th century were found. They are to be seen on the right-hand side of the road. Further on to the right is the historic inn Zur letzten Instanz (16th century), and to the left on Parochialstrasse stands the great **Parochialkirche** (1695–1714), which was damaged in the war.

Turn right into Klosterstrasse, where the remains of the **Klosterkirche** can be seen. It belonged to the Franciscan order of monks known as the Graue Brüder (Grey Brothers). From 1574 onwards, the monastery housed the oldest school in Brandenburg, the Berlinische Gymnasium zum Grauen Kloster, whose most famous pupil was Bismarck.

Turkish delights on Alexanderplatz

Grunerstrasse leads to **Alexanderplatz** or 'Alex' for short. The east German authorities created a new but rather uninviting town centre around this square. This vast, often windswept space is dominated by the **Fernsehturm** (television tower), which was completed in 1969. It is 365m (1,100ft) high, and described by Berliners as the *Tele-Spargel* (Tele-asparagus). There is a fine view of Berlin from the observation platform which is in the lower half of the steel sphere at a height of 203m (600ft). The Tele Café above it revolves once every hour. The **World Time Clock** is a popular meeting place for young people as is the **Brunnen der Völkerfreundschaft** (Fountain of International Friendship). This square, which in the 1920s and 1930s had been one of the most vibrant parts of the city, will soon see its skyline change again as a new scheme by the Berlin architect Hans Kollhof takes shape.

The Television Tower

Karl-Marx-Allee – known as Stalinallee until 1961 – and its extension, Frankfurterallee, runs east for about 5km (3 miles), bordered by Soviet-style tenement blocks of between six and nine storeys. This, the longest street in the city and preserved as a 'document to Berlin's postwar history' is a depressing sight. It will be some time before life returns to the 'avenue of no customers and no shops'.

Route 4

Around the ★★ Zoo and the ★ Kurfürstendamm

This tour begins at a major landmark in the west of the city, the Bahnhof Zoologischer Garten or simply Zoo station. It is also a U-Bahn and an S-Bahn station as well as a departure point for several bus routes and BVG coach tours. The station, which was run by the Deutsche Reichsbahn (East German railway company), has been in decline for many years, although it was only renovated in 1987. Drug addicts and dealers, alcoholics, petty criminals and vagrants have made the station their home, and rail travellers are frequently confronted by a depressing picture of human misery.

Survival struggles of quite a different kind – and in much more beautiful surroundings – take place just opposite the station, in ★★ The Zoo **⑬** (daily 9am–6.30pm). Entrance DM 9, children aged 3–15 DM 4.50. Combined tickets for the zoo and aquarium DM 13.50, children DM 6.50. There is another entrance in Budapester Strasse, which also leads directly to the aquarium.

The Zoo is the oldest in Germany

Berlin Zoo, set in 33ha (80 acres), was founded in 1841 and is the oldest zoo in Germany, and ninth oldest in the world after Vienna, Paris, London, Dublin, Bristol, Manchester, Amsterdam and Antwerp. It was almost destroyed during the bombardment of 23 November 1943 and only 93 animals survived. Now there are 1,600 different species and about 14,000 mammals and birds all told, making it the most extensive and impressive collection of animals in the world.

The main attractions are the carnivores, which enjoy the biggest enclosure in the world, a delightful section

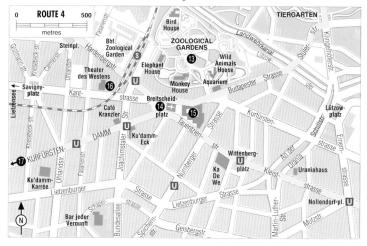

The giraffes and some even more exotic ornamentation

The Aquarium: facade detail

for nocturnal animals (underground), the bird house and the bear enclosure.

The giant panda from China is the public's favourite. Named Bao Bao, it is the only panda in Germany. The monkey house includes some remarkable breeds, such as gorillas, orang-utans and proboscis monkeys. The rhinoceros and elephant houses are worth a visit, but the marvellous setting for the zoo has become a tourist attraction in its own right. Old trees, beautiful expanses of green, ponds and streams, not to mention the restaurants and children's play areas, create an ideal destination for a day out. In 1987, a new 21,000-sq m (25,000-sq yd) enclosure was opened on the other side of the Landwehrkanal. But this zoo is still much smaller than Friedrichsfeld Zoo in the eastern half of the city, which has half the number of animals but five times the space.

Built in 1913 and renovated in 1980, the Berlin ★★ **Aquarium** is the biggest in Europe (daily 9am–6pm, last Saturday of the month 9am–9pm). Entrance DM 8, children DM 4. The Aquarium contains about 600 different species with about 8,520 creatures in all. Many of the displays have been specially constructed to recreate complete natural landscapes with rivers, fish and reptiles; crocodiles and alligators live in their natural habitat. The insect house contains a marvellous collection of arthropods (centipedes, spiders, scorpions, etc) from all parts of the world.

Outside on Budapester Strasse 42, the **Staatliche Kunsthalle** (State Art Gallery), is a leading exhibition centre. It is chiefly devoted to displaying the work of contemporary artists, but now and then it does stage notable retrospectives.

The **Kaiser-Wilhelm-Gedächtniskirche (Memorial Church) ⓮** on Breitscheidtplatz is impossible to miss. Franz Schwechten built the Gedächtniskirche in neo-

Romanesque style between 1891–5 and dedicated it to Kaiser William I, but it is also a memorial to Bismarck and to the founding of the German Reich. The church was partially destroyed in World War II and a long dispute about whether it should be restored or demolished was settled by a compromise: the tower (68m/200ft) or 'The Hollow Tooth' as Berliners call it, would remain as a ruined monument, but a new church would be built around it.

Kaiser William Memorial Church

Between 1959–61, Egon Eiermann built a number of adjoining sections which consisted of an octagonal main building, a small chapel and a 53-m (150-ft) six-sided tower. Each of the eight walls of the octagon consists of up to 300 small, blue, square glass mosaics from Chartres. The belltower plays a tune composed by Prince Louis Ferdinand of Prussia (1907–1994). Eiermann's work merely prolonged the controversy about the church among Berliners, who nicknamed the new church the 'Soul Silo'. Difficult problems still remain: the ruined tower is continuing to crumble and the modern concrete honeycomb structure will have to be restored.

Opened in 1965, the neighbouring **Europa Center** 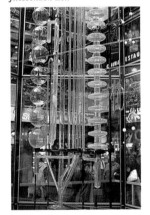 is the biggest shopping, commercial and entertainment centre in Berlin. It houses over 100 shops, cafés, bars and restaurants, five cinemas, die Stachelschweine cabaret, the Palace Hotel, La Vie en Rose revue theatre and die Thermen sauna baths. It is well worth the effort to take a lift to the viewing platform at the top of the 20-storey tower for the ★ **panorama of Berlin**. The Kleine Spielbank with 100 games machines is in the Hotel Steigenberger (*see page 102*).

Europa Center: Uhr der fliessenden Zeit

In May 1982, a much admired curiosity was unveiled on the ground floor of the Europa Center: the **Uhr der fliessenden Zeit** is a 13-m (40-ft) high water clock. It was created by a French physicist called Gitton for people who have no need for a watch but who enjoy watching time pass. In 1984, Joachim Schmettau built the **Weltkugelbrunnen** (fountain of the globe) in front of the Europa Center. Berliners call it Wasserklops (water meatball).

Weltkugelbrunnen

Kantstrasse runs westward from Breitscheidplatz, becoming Neue Kantstrasse as it extends into the district of Charlottenburg, towards the International Congress Centre (ICC) and the Exhibition Halls (*see page 51*). On the right-hand side just before Fasanenstrasse is the **Theater des Westens**, which was built in 1895 and 1896 and has been lavishly renovated.

A little further along is Savignyplatz, which is dotted with *Kneipen*, cafés and shops. This is a popular area, especially for pubs and for 'alternative' bookshops, which can even be found under the arches of the S-Bahn viaduct.

Behind Wilhelmsdorfer Strasse, Charlottenburg's main shopping street, Neue Kantstrasse crosses the Liet-

The reclusive Lietzenseepark

The exclusive Ka De We

Chic hotels on the Ku'damm

zenseepark, 10ha (25 acres) of delightful parkland which surround the Lietzensee with its restaurant and rowing boats for hire. Neue Kantstrasse ends at Messedamm by the ICC (International Conference Centre).

Taking a southeasterly route from Breitscheidplatz is **Tauentzienstrasse**, an extension to the Kurfürstendamm. It is Berlin's main shopping street, where, just before Wittenbergplatz on the Schöneberg side, the Kaufhaus des Westens or Ka De We (*see page 90*), one of the most exclusive department stores in Europe, can be found. The food counter, one of the biggest in the world, should not be missed. Over on the other side of Wittenbergplatz, the 'Tauentzien', as Berliners call it for short, becomes Kleiststrasse, where the Uraniahaus has lectures, films and slideshows during the day on political, historical, artistic and health-related topics.

The ★ **Kurfürstendamm**, which leads almost due west from Breitscheidplatz, was once the route that the Elector took from his residence on the Spreeinsel to his hunting lodge in the Grunewald. For centuries, this boulevard was a track across the fields, through sand and marsh, until in 1871 Bismarck set his eyes on the Champs Elysées in Paris. The Iron Chancellor became obsessed with plans for a similar mighty avenue for the capital of the newly formed German Empire. In 1875, construction work began, and by May 1886 steam-driven street cars began running between Grunewald and the zoo. The street cars did not last for long, but what has lasted since the 1930s is the Ku'damm myth which expresses itself in an undefined longing called 'homesickness for the Kurfürstendamm'.

In World War II, over 200 of the 250 houses were destroyed or badly damaged on the 3.5-km (2-mile) stretch as far as the Halenseebrücke. The few remaining buildings which have now been fully restored with their cupolas, extravagant decoration and magnificent doorways reflect the Wilhelmenian splendour of those times. There is a story that the Berlin workman would approach his master and say: 'Sir, the house is ready. What style would you like it finished in?'

Now, 100 years later, the Ku'damm is still one of the finest boulevards in Germany, a place for Berliners to stroll, to see and be seen. In this respect, Unter den Linden and Friedrichstrasse in the east offer little competition because of the shortage of shops and restaurants. The Ku'damm has, however, lost some of its exclusive feel as 'Europe's biggest café', but its character is now expressed in different ways. It has become classless, some say it attracts undesirable elements; It is true, there has been much controversy about the fact that street traders and fast-food stands have taken over the pavements and that the traditional, up-market businesses have been forced to move into the side streets to let in the only retailers who can afford to pay the enormous rents – the department stores, chain stores, sex shows and cheap bars. But the side streets, where the pace is less hectic than on the Ku'damm, are now well established. They have benefited as a range of interesting shops have opened along with pleasant pubs and cafés. However, there is still something special about the Ku'damm: many of the top hotels, restaurants and cafés have stayed put, including exclusive haute couture shops and, antique dealers and many theatres, such as the famous **Schaubühne** 🄻, which has found a new home on Lehniner Platz.

At the junction with Joachimstaler Strasse is the new **Café Kranzler**. Kranzler-Ecke, or Kranzler corner, where Unter den Linden meets Friedrichstrasse, was a well-known meeting place for the rich and famous in pre-war days. Another shopping centre is the Ku'damm Karree, which is built around the Theater am Kurfürstendamm and the Komödie and situated between the Kurfürstendamm and Uhlandstrasse.

Café Kranzler

At Fasanenstrasse 24, next to the marvellous Literaturhaus café, with its wonderful garden, is the **Käthe Kollwitz Museum**. On display is a comprehensive collection of drawings, sculptures and graphics by the artist Käthe Kollwitz (1867–1945); her work dealt with tragic subjects and had a strong social or political content. The restored Villa Grisebach (Fasanenstrasse 25) organises fine art auctions for an international clientele twice a year and during the rest of the year it houses the highly-regarded Galerie Pels-Leusden. Between Fasanenstrasse and Uhlandstrasse lies an up-market shopping mall with a number of restaurants inside a courtyard.

Käthe Kollwitz, the artist

For people who have time for arithmetic, there is the **Mengenlehre-uhr** (teaching clock) on the traffic island at the junction of the Kurfürstendamm and Uhlandstrasse.

Escaping the bustle

Route 5

Zoo station – Ernst-Reuter-Platz – Tiergarten

The Jewish Community Centre

This route starts off from the Zoo station, and proceeds along Hardenbergstrasse in a northwesterly direction. The first building on the right is the Federal Court. Jebenstrasse runs along the side of the station and at number 2 is the building that, until recently, housed the Kunstbibliothek Berlin (Berlin Arts Library), which has now moved to the Art Forum at Matthaikirchplatz (*see page 42*).

Continue along Hardenbergstrasse to Fasanenstrasse. On the right, on the corner of Hardenberg and Fasanenstrasse, is the **Hochschule der Künste**, one of Germany's top colleges for music, art, design and architecture. Its concert hall is a modern glass building with room for 1,360 people and a theatre auditorium. In the foyer is Hans Uhlmann's sculpture *Concerto*. Many well-known artists teach at the college, which has 5,500 students.

On the left in Fasanenstrasse (Nos 79–80) is the **Jewish Community Centre ⑱**. This centre was rebuilt in 1959 on the site of the synagogue which was destroyed during the Kristallnacht in 1938, when Nazi stormtroopers took to the streets, vandalising and destroying Jewish synagogues, shops and other properties. The doorway and the remains of some of the pillars which were saved from the old synagogue have been incorporated into the new building. A sculpture of one of the destroyed scriptures stands on a plinth in front of the building. This community centre is the cultural focal point for Berlin's Jewish community, which is one of the largest in Germany with more than 10,000 members.

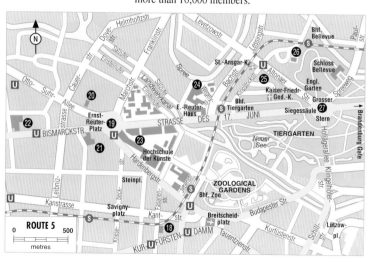

On Steinplatz is a memorial to the victims of National Socialism. It is carved from stones which were rescued from the ruined synagogue in Fasanenstrasse; another memorial recalls the victims of Stalinism. The cafés and *Kneipen* around Steinplatz have become the haunts of Berlin's student community. Stretching from opposite Steinplatz as far as Ernst-Reuter-Platz is the Technische Universität (TU).

Past the Renaissance-Theater, formerly August Gaul's Entenbrunnen (1911), on the other side of the road, is **Ernst-Reuter-Platz** ⓳, where Strasse des 17. Juni meets Hardenbergstrasse. One of the busiest squares for traffic in the city, it is dominated by modern office blocks and the new Technische Universität buildings. In Marchstrasse is a 5-m (15-ft) high sculpture by Bernhard Heiliger called *Die Flamme* (The Flame) dedicated to Ernst Reuter, a former mayor of West Berlin.

Near Ernst-Reuter-Platz in Otto-Suhr-Allee is the small **Tribüne Theater** ⓴ and in Bismarckstrasse stands the **Schiller Theater** ㉑. Once one of Berlin's leading theatres, it now shows famous musicals. A little further along Bismarckstrasse, on the other side of the road, is the **★ Deutsche Oper Berlin** ㉒. One of three opera houses in the city, this was designed by Fritz Bornemann in 1961. In front of the 70-m (220-ft) long facade of pebble-dashed concrete slabs, stands an **abstract sculpture** by Hans Uhlmann (1961).

Almost 3km (2 miles) long, Strasse des 17. Juni runs east from Ernst-Reuter-Platz to the Brandenburg Gate (*see page 14*). On the right are the main buildings of the **Technische Universität** ㉓. The modern Technical University developed from the Königlich-Technischen Hochschule (Royal Technical College) which was founded in 1879. It is the oldest college in West Berlin and since World War II it has incorporated many new departments which stretch

Schiller Theatre: doorway detail

Memorial to victims of Stalinism

37

Sculpture by Hans Uhlmann

from Fasanenstrasse to the other side of Strasse des 17. Juni as far as the Einstein-Ufer (Heinrich-Hertz-Institut). As well as the technical and scientific faculty, a philosophy faculty was added in 1950. A total of some 35,000 students attend the TU.

Strasse des 17. Juni crosses the Landwehrkanal by the Charlottenburger bridge, decorated with bronze statues of King Frederick I and Queen Sophie Charlotte. On the left is Ernst-Reuter-Haus, which is home to the Senate library, the German Institute for Urban Studies and the Berlin office of the Association of Municipal Authorities. Just before Tiergarten S-Bahn station on the left is Wegelystrasse, the site of the **National Porcelain Factory** ㉔. W C Wegely founded the first Berlin porcelain factory in 1751 and it was then acquired by Frederick the Great for the Prussian state. The blue sceptre of the Brandenburg Electorate is still displayed as a trademark of what was the Königliche-Porzellan-Manufaktur or KPM (Royal Porcelain Factory). The exhibition rooms in Wegelystrasse and salerooms at Kurfürstendamm 205 are open Monday to Friday 9am–6pm, Saturday 9am–2pm.

Romancing in the English Garden

Stretching along both sides of the Strasse des 17. Juni between the Tiergarten S-Bahn station and the Brandenburg Gate is the ★ **Tiergarten.** This splendid park was once a royal hunting ground and enclosure for wild animals and is about 3km (2 miles) long by 1km wide. A century ago, the famous landscape gardener Peter Joseph Lenné (1789–1866) turned this area into one of the most beautiful parks in Europe. Lenné's distinctive style is still recognisable among the shaded avenues, lakes and watercourses with their small bridges.

During the wars and in the subsequent years, the Tiergarten was devastated; all trees were cut down and the land cultivated. Ernst Reuter, Berlin's mayor, laid the foundations for the new Tiergarten in 1949 when he planted the first linden tree at the Grosser Stern by the Siegessäule (Victory Column). Since then, over a million trees and shrubs have been planted and the Tiergarten with 25km (15 miles) of footpaths is now one of Berlin's most attractive areas. The most popular haunts in the park are the Neue See with its café and rowing boats for hire, the Rose Garden and the English Garden which was donated by Queen Elizabeth II and opened by the then foreign minister Anthony Eden.

Sculpture in the Tiergarten

Lying to the north of the Tiergarten is an architectural original: the ★ **Hansaviertel** ㉕. No other part of Berlin was so extensively destroyed in World War II as the area between Tiergarten and Bellevue S-Bahn stations. It had to be completely cleared and, in 1957, 48 architects from 13 countries (including Walter Gropius, Alvar Aalto and Oscar Niemeyer) took part in an international architectural exhibition in which they displayed their innovative designs for a model residential estate.

The residences ranged from detached one-family houses to blocks of flats. Also specially designed were the Protestant Kaiser-Friedrich Memorial Church, the Catholic St Angars Church (whose bells were donated by the German Chancellor Konrad Adenauer), a school, a library, shops, restaurants, its own U-Bahn station (Hansaplatz) and a children's theatre. In the aftermath of 1968, the now famous **Grips Theatre** had a profound influence on progressive children's and youth theatre throughout Europe. A sign outside each house indicates the name of the relevant architect.

St Angar's Church

Adjacent to the English Garden is the **Akademie der Künste (Academy of Arts)** ❷❻. This institution follows on in the tradition of the first Prussian arts academy, which the Elector Frederick III created in 1696 as the third such academy in Europe after Rome and Paris. In 1969, German-American benefactor Henry H Reichold made a donation which enabled Berlin architect Werner Düttman to go ahead with his plans. This academy, whose aim is to encourage architecture, music, literature, the fine arts and the performing arts, and to keep the public informed on contemporary artistic developments, has gone on to become one of the leading cultural centres in Berlin. In 1993, it merged with its counterpart in the eastern part of the city.

39

The academy consists of an exhibition hall, a studio and auditorium and another building with a workshop, lounge and conference room. The exhibitions are changed on a regular basis. At the main entrance stands a Henry Moore sculpture called *Die Liegende* (Reclining Woman).

Henry Moore's Reclining Woman

After viewing the Hansaviertel, follow Altonaer Strasse past the English Garden as far as the Grosser Stern roundabout. In the middle is the **Siegessäule (Victory Column)** ❷❼. Its viewing platform is open Tuesday to Sunday 9am–6pm; closed during snowy and icy weather.

The Victory Column

The Siegessäule was built in accordance with Heinrich Strack's plans in 1873 to commemorate the Prussian campaigns against Denmark (1864), Austria (1866) and France (1870–1). The column was first built in Königsplatz but it was moved and rebuilt where it is now. The addition of a square granite base raised its height from 61m (180ft) to 67m (200ft). A glass mosaic by the emperor's favourite painter Anton von Werner, which represents the 19th-century wars for German freedom and unity, is housed in the 16-pillared rotunda. The latter serves as a pedestal for the sandstone tower which is decorated with French gun barrels. It is crowned with Drake's gilded goddess of victory, *Viktoria*, which is 8.3m (26ft) tall and weighs 350kg (750lb). The 50-m (150-ft) high ★ **viewing platform** offers a splendid view of the Brandenburg Gate and across to Alexanderplatz.

Route 6

Schloss Bellevue

40

*The fourth largest
belltower in the world*

Take the Spreeweg from the Grosser Stern roundabout past Schlosspark Bellevue to **Schloss Bellevue ㉘**. The palace was built by Michael Philipp Boumann in 1785 for Prince Ferdinand, the youngest brother of Frederick the Great, with Carl Langhans designing the interior. It was badly damaged during World War II, but rebuilding work started in 1954 and included renovation of the Classical, oval room known as the Langhans-Saal. Since the end of 1993, the building has served as the official seat of the German President.

The **Kongresshalle (Congress Hall) ㉙** was built in 15 months with money provided by the Benjamin Franklin Foundation as the American contribution to the 'Interbau 57' competition. The architect, Hugh A Stubbins, won plaudits throughout Europe for his adventurous design, but the Berliners christened it the 'Pregnant Oyster' on account of its vaulted roof, which resembles an inverted oyster shell. In 1980 part of the roof collapsed and the building was not reopened until 1987. It is now home to the *Haus der Kulturen der Welt* (House of World Cultures), which encourages world-wide links by offering international theatre, dance, film, etc to the German people. Situated between the Kongresshalle and the Reichstag is the Carillon belltower which with its 68 bells is the fourth largest in the world. The bells play for five minutes every day at noon and 6pm.

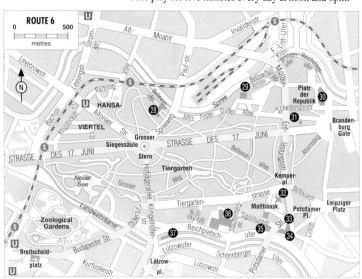

John-Foster-Dulles Allee leads to Platz der Republik. On the western side is the site of the building where Hitler's Reichstag sat but it was demolished in 1951. New government buildings are planned for this area, eg the Federal Chancellor's office will be built on the south bank of the Spree. To the east of the Platz der Republic, directly on the line of the old Wall, stands the **Reichstag** ㉚. The Reichstag was built between 1884 and 1894 by Paul Wallot in the Italian Renaissance style. It was badly damaged by fire in 1933 and then in 1945 it was totally destroyed by Allied bombs. Between 1957 and 1971 it was rebuilt but without its dome.

The Reichstag with its glass dome by Sir Norman Foster

In October 1990, the Reichstag was the focal point of the spectacular celebrations marking the reunification of Germany and on 4 November that year, after an interval of 57 years, the full German parliament convened here again. In June 1995 Berlin had a three-week party when the Reichstag was entirely covered in tarpaulin. After that, the London architect Sir Norman Foster crowned the war-damaged building with a delicate glass dome as the modern counterpart of the lost original.

Just south of the Platz der Republik stands the **Soviet Memorial** ㉛. Built in 1946, it overlooks Strasse des 17. Juni. From the Platz der Republik it is just a short walk to the Brandenburg Gate and the famous Unter den Linden (*see page 15*).

41

The Soviet Memorial

For the moment, however, follow the relief road from the Reichstag to the south as far as Kemperplatz on the southern edge of the Tiergarten, where the late classical Matthäuskirche is situated (built in 1846 and restored in 1958). Leading off Kemperplatz is Bellevuestrasse, which leads to Potsdamer Platz. Here, Berlin seems to be leading the way into the future: Europe's largest inner-city building site at Potsdamer Platz has now become a favourite tourist spot, second only to the Brandenburg Gate. Companies such as Daimler Benz, ABB and Sony have built a huge high-rise complex with offices. There are 600 flats, a musical theatre, the Grand Hyatt Hotel, a cinema centre and the Spielbank Berlin, a casino with roulette, baccarat and black jack (daily 2pm–3am). The red Info-Box, a striking building at Leipziger Platz 21, houses an exhibition about the history of the place. The platform on the upper floor offers a veiw of the whole area.

The Philharmonie

The development to the south of Kemperplatz, known as the the **Kulturforum**, has become an important area for museums and cultural centres. First, there is the distinctive **Philharmonie (Philharmonic Hall)** ㉜. The new home for the Berlin Philharmonic Orchestra was built between 1960 and 1963 according to Hans Scharoun's design. The ochre-coloured octagon with its tent-like roof represents one of the most exciting developments in mod-

Museum of Musical Instruments and the Lüneberg treasures

Dante's 'Divine Comedy' in the Kuppppferstichkabinett

ern architecture. The main concert hall itself is 60m (200ft) long, 55m (170ft) wide and 21m (65ft) high, is reckoned to have superb acoustics and can accommodate 2,200 people. The smaller Kammermusiksaal or chamber music hall (again based on Scharoun's design) with seats for 1,000 was opened in 1987.

On one side of the Philharmonie is the **Musikinstrumentenmuseum (Museum of Musical Instruments)** which opened in 1984. On the other side is the ★ **Kunstgewerbemuseum (Museum of Arts and Crafts)**, which displays a wealth of European arts and crafts from the early Middle Ages (★ Guelfic treasures, Carolingian and Romanesque church treasures), the Renaissance (★ Lüneberg civic treasures, Italian and Spanish majiolica), the baroque period (glassware, faience pottery), the turn of the century (*Jugendstil* or art nouveau) right through to today. The latest addition to the Kulturforum is the **Painting Gallery**, which was completed in 1998. The modern cube with its entrance at Sigismundstrasse houses a brilliant collection of around 700 paintings, which give an overview of the development of European painting from the 13th century up to the Baroque period.

At Matthäuskirchplatz 6 is the ★★ **Berliner Kupferstichkabinett (Prints and Drawings Collection)** ㉝. It is by far the finest of all German collections of graphic art, and ranks fourth in the world behind London, Paris and Vienna. The wealth of drawings is outstanding, especially in German and Dutch works. There is a superb collection of drawings by ★ Rembrandt and ★ Dürer, and many others by Holbein the Younger, Grünewald, Altdorfer and Cranach. The best Rembrandt collection in the world is in Berlin. The same is true of the drawings by ★★ Antoine Watteau, a leading French artist. Further highlights of the collection are the etchings by the German Impres-

sionists Liebermann, Corinth and Slevogt and the Expressionist group, *Die Brücke* (*see also page 58*). There is a wide collection of Pop Art originals, which can be viewed in the study room on request.

The same building houses the **Kunstbibliothek Berlin (Berlin Arts Library)**. The National Library of the Foundation for Prussian Cultural Heritage, to give it its full name, is the home of 180,000 books and documents relating to the history of Prussian fine art. It contains the Lipperheidesche Kostümbibliothek with some 16,000 volumes and 60,000 drawings of traditional costumes, the Graphische Sammlung (a collection of hand drawings and engravings from the Gothic period to modern times), the Sammlung Grisebach (documents the history of European book design) and the Gebrauchsgraphik- and Plakatsammlung, containing around 100,000 pages of commercial art and posters.

The **Staatsbibliothek (National Library)** ③, is situated in the Potsdamer Strasse, and was designed by Hans Scharoun and completed in 1978. In 1992 it was amalgamated with the Deutsche Staatsbibliothek in Unter den Linden to become Berlin's Staatsbibliothek–Preussischer Kulturbesitz, the Centre for Prussian Culture. Over 10 million volumes tell the history of the city and environs.

National Gallery: Bearing the Cross by Baselitz

43

The ★ **Neue Nationalgalerie (New National Gallery)** ③ was designed by Mies van der Rohe and opened in 1968. It contains one of the most impressive collections of 19th- and 20th-century art. The German Romantics, French and German Impressionists and the German Expressionists are all well represented. Works by Max Ernst, Francis Bacon, Lam and Matta are the highlights for those who enjoy surrealistic art, but there are also paintings by contemporary artists such as Penck and Kiefer. Also on display are the works of such celebrated sculptors as Henry Moore, Schadow, Rodin, Barlach, Maillol and Scheibe.

About five minutes walk from the Nationalgalerie at Stauffenbergstrasse 13–14 is the **Gedenkstätte für Opfer des 20. Juli 1944 (Memorial to German Resistance)** ③. It was in this building, the Supreme Army Command, that the unsuccessful attempt on Hitler's life took place in July 1944. Several senior army officers including Beck, Olbricht, Graf von Stauffenberg and Henning von Fresckow were court-martialled and shot immediately after the assassination attempt. In 1953, a monument designed by Richard Scheibe was erected in the courtyard of the building in memory of these officers.

By the Landwehrkanal is the **Bauhaus Archiv** ③, one of the Berlin-born architect Walter Gropius' later designs. Gropius had always wanted his work to be admired in Berlin itself.

Bauhaus Archiv

Route 7

★ Schloss Charlottenburg

Schloss Charlottenburg

The entrance to Schloss Charlottenburg is in Luisenplatz, opposite an old milestone (c 1800) with the inscription '*1 Meile von Berlin*', ie 7.5km (about 4 miles) from Donhöffplatz which was then regarded as the centre of Berlin. Facing the Schloss (palace) on either side of Schlossstrasse stand two identical barrack-style buildings. To the west is the **Berggruen Collection** and to the east is the Ägyptisches Museum (Egyptian Museum; *see page 46*). Both these buildings were constructed between 1851 and 1859 by one of Schinkel's pupils, Friedrich August Schiller.

The finest and biggest palace in the city is undoubtedly ★ **Schloss Charlottenburg** ㊳. It was designed by the master builder Arnold Nering, having been commissioned originally as a country house in 1695 by the countess and later Queen of Prussia, Sophie Charlotte. The Swedish architect, Eosander von Göthe, made some significant changes between 1701 and 1712. It was greatly enlarged with the addition of a 48-m (150-ft) dome above the main building and an orangery on the western side. Another orangery was planned for the eastern side but this never materialised.

When Frederick the Great ascended to the throne in 1740, responsibility for the design of the east wing, the 'New Wing', was given to Georg Wenzeslaus von Knobelsdorff. Frederick William II, who succeeded Frederick the Great in 1786, then commissioned Carl Gotthard Langhans to build the theatre and the Belvedere tea-house. The latter was destroyed in 1943 but has been faithfully restored. In 1952, Schlüter's famous 1697 statue, the *Reiterdenkmal des Grossen Kurfürst* (Great Elector on Horseback), was erected in the main courtyard. The statue had originally stood on the Lange Brücke (now called the Rathausbrücke) near Berlin's Stadtschloss (city palace) in the heart of the city. Schlüter's work – a replica of which is in the Bode Museum – is the considered by many to be the finest monument from the German baroque period.

The palace's **Historical Rooms** have been fully restored and may be visited (Tuesday to Friday 9am–5pm, Saturday and Sunday 10am–5pm). The rooms on the ground floor of the Nering/Eosander section of the palace may only be visited as part of a conducted tour.

Along the main corridor, the Frederick I room and Sophie Charlotte room are open for viewing; both are very sumptuously furnished mainly with Chinese furniture in the style of the period. In many of the rooms there are paintings by the French portrait artist Antoine Pesne, who had been summoned to the Prussian court in 1710 by Frederick I. The ★ **porcelain room** contains an extremely impressive collection of Chinese porcelain.

Watteau painting

The finest rooms in Knobelsdorff's **New Wing** in the east are on the upper floor. Frederick the Great's luxuriously furnished living rooms are further enhanced by the ★★ paintings of Antoine Watteau, who, together with Lancret and Pater, was greatly admired by the king. Schloss Charlottenburg houses the biggest collection of Watteau's paintings outside France. The Weisse Saal (White Room), the king's dining room and the Goldene Galerie (Golden Gallery), Knobelsdorff's enormous banqueting hall, have all now been fully restored. The latter is one of the very finest examples of German rococo design and well worth a visit.

Until 1985, the Kunstgewerbemuseum (Museum of Arts and Crafts), which was founded in 1867, occupied the ground floor in Schloss Charlottenburg and was one of richest and largest of its kind in Germany. However, in 1985, the Kunstgewerbemuseum moved to new premises in Tiergarten (*see page 42*).

New Wing: rococo detail

Its rooms have now been taken over by the **Galerie der Romantik**. This section of the Nationalgalerie has a fine display of sculptures from the Romantic and Biedermeier period and also paintings by Caspar David Friedrich which belong to the national palaces and gardens collection.

The original palace theatre, the Langhans building in the west, houses the **Museum für Vor- und Frühgeschichte (Museum of Ancient and Early History)**, which suffered very badly in World War II. Some important finds by the famous German archaeologist Heinrich Schliemann were lost. As well as some locally discovered artefacts, the museum also houses European and Middle Eastern exhibits dating from the Stone Age, the Bronze Age and the early and late Iron Age.

The **Belvedere tea-house** in the palace gardens was built by Langhans in 1788 for Frederick William II and contains a porcelain collection. Also worth looking out for in the English-style landscaped park is the Mausoleum which Schinkel designed for Luise and Frederick William III, but Kaiser William I and his queen Augusta also lie buried there.

Schinkel Pavilion and sculpture

The **Schinkel Pavilion**, which is modelled on a Neapolitan villa, was built in 1824 and 1825. It was later restored and in 1970 became a museum housing some of Schinkel's drawings and, plans, in addition to a collection of sculptures, paintings and objets d'art that date from his time. The pavilion also holds some rare pictures of

The Berggruen Collection

*Egyptian Museum:
view into the cupola*

*Bust of
Nefertiti*

the great architect. In front of the building on two bronze pillars stands Christian Daniel Rauch's notable sculpture, *Viktorien*.

Apart from the Museum of Ancient and Early History, the district of Charlottenburg has two other very important collections – the Berggruen Collection and the Egyptian Museum. Both collections are housed in buildings designed by Friedrich August Stüler.

Since 1996, the **Berggruen Collection** has housed approximately 100 paintings, sculptures and drawings by eight artists of worldwide renown: Picasso, Klee, Cézanne, Matisse, van Gogh, Braque, Laurens and Giacometti. Heinz Berggruen, the Jewish collector and fine art dealer, who grew up in Germany and spent the majority of his life in the USA, loaned his valuable collection to Berlin for at least 10 years and has thus filled a void left behind by the iconoclasm of the National socialists (*see page 82*).

The ★ **Ägyptisches Museum (Egyptian Museum)**, situated at Schlossstrasse 70, houses treasures dating from between around 500 BC and AD 300. However, the museum only displays artefacts that were stored in the West during the war. Work is currently taking place on the war-damaged New Museum on the Museum Island, and once this building has been restored, the entire collection of Egyptian treasures, including a notable collection of small Egyptian sculptures, will be housed there.

The Nile Valley exhibits date from 4500BC until the days of the Roman Empire. The museum's pride and joy is the ★★★ *Bust of Nefertiti*, which was found in 1912 in Tell el-Amarna. It is 48cm (20in) tall and dates from around 1350BC. Also of special interest are the ★ ebony carving of Queen Teje (about 1370BC), the *Berlin Green Head,* one of the best examples of later Egyptian sculpture (600–330BC), and the ★★ *Kalbasha Monumental Gate,* a gift to the museum from the former Egyptian President Sadat, which is on display in the old royal stables.

The **Bröhan Museum** (*see page 82*) is situated next to the Berggruen Museum and houses collections of paintings, graphic art, sculpture, glass and pottery, which date from the *Jugendstil* period (the German interpretation of art nouveau) of the end of the 19th century to the stylised art deco style of the 1920s and 1930s. The rooms in the museum are all named after leading art nouveau and art deco designers and cabinetmakers and include such inspirational figures as Hector Guimard and Louis Majorelle.

In nearby Sophie-Charlotten-Strasse 17–18 is the **National Plaster Casting Company**. A veritable treasure trove for statue lovers, this is where replicas of all the well-known statues and busts on view in museums throughout the world may be purchased.

Route 8

Berlin-Mitte – Prenzlauer Berg *See map on page 26*

*Tacheles Culture Centre,
Oranienburger Strasse*

Depressing though **Alexanderplatz** itself may be, its hinterland is actually full of life. Here, in the heart of **Berlin-Mitte**, a thriving district of artists and pubs has developed, an urban idyll caught between the ruins and the renovations of the past.

This route begins at the S-Bahn station Hackescher Markt, to the west of Alexanderplatz, where, in Rosen-thaler Strasse, between Sophienstrasse and Oranienburger Strasse, are the **Hackesche Höfe** (courtyards). When they were built in 1906, they were famous as the largest residential and trading estate in Germany. They give a good impression of life in Berlin in the early 20th century, although they offered a much better living environment than the crowded tenement blocks that had sprung up on the fringes of the city since industrialisation began. The first of the eight courtyards has a brick facade decorated with colourful art nouveau ornamentation. Today, a number of cultural facilities have established themselves in the area, including the Chamäleon variety club and the Sophienclub with its café and restaurant.

In Oranienburger Strasse, which begins at Hackescher Markt, stands the **Synagogue**. When it was built in 1866, it was the largest and most magnificent synagogue in the city. It was destroyed not by the Nazis but by the Allied bombs of World War II and has since been reconstructed. Since work on the interior was completed in 1995, the synagogue has housed the *Centrum Judaicum*, documenting Jewish life in Berlin and Brandenburg.

New perspectives

The Synagogue

Jewish culture returns

In its cultural heyday at the end of the 19th century, Berlin had the biggest and most influential Jewish community in Europe. Around 180,000 Jews lived in the city until they were eradicated by the Nazis. Oranienburger Strasse and the surrounding streets form the old Jewish district of Berlin known as the **Scheunenviertel**. In the 1920s, it was in this district that many east European Jews, fleeing from persecution, found a new home. Before the Nazis arrived on the scene, it was a bustling area awash with cultural vitality. Now, beneath the gleaming cupola of the synagogue, some of the old way of life is returning – not just a multicultural mix of cultural events and entertainment, but also a new and vital Jewish lifestyle: Scheunviertel has emerged as one of Berlin's liveliest quarters in no time at all, and on this account alone, the area is definitely worth spending some time in.

In the side streets, such as Tucholskystrasse, but particularly in Oranienburger Strasse itself, a number of kosher restaurants and cafés have established themselves.

Scheunenviertel is a district of artists and galleries

Housed in an old department store, **Tacheles** in Oranienburger Strasse is a thriving cultural centre; in the narrow **Auguststrasse** a growing art scene has emerged, with galleries for young artists.

Sophienstrasse was restored in the days of the GDR. Here lies the **Sophienkirche** (1712–32), the only remaining baroque church in the city. In the churchyard are the graves of the composer Carl Friedrich Zelter, the historian Leopold von Ranke and the poetess Anna Luise Karsch. Entrance to the church is via the Grosser Hamburger Strasse, erstwhile location of the Jewish old people's home and Berlin's oldest Jewish cemetery (memorial tablet to Moses Mendelssohn). In 1942, the Nazis used the old people's home as an assembly camp, from which they deported 55,000 Jews to Auschwitz and Theresienstadt.

Rather like the district of Kreuzberg in the west, the working-class district of **Prenzlauer Berg** has developed its own sub-culture. Of all the old tenement blocks with their narrow, dark courtyards in the eastern half of the city, 40 percent are in Prenzlauer Berg. Most of them date from the period 1850–1900 and are in a poor state of repair. A few streets were restored in advance of the city's 750th anniversary celebrations in 1987, including Husemannstrasse and Kollwitzplatz. The **Jewish Cemetery** in Schönhauser Allee contains the graves of influential personalities from Berlin's past cultural, economic and political life.

Part of the Prenzelberg scenery

The Prenzelberg scene, a mixture of young workers, students, intellectuals, artists and writers, comes together in the district's cafés. In the 1980s, the **Gethsemene Church** in Stargarder Strasse achieved fame as a meeting point for GDR opposition activists.

Route 9

Kreuzberg

In terms of area, **Kreuzberg** is Berlin's second smallest district, but at the same time it is the most densely populated. The population, made up predominantly of workers, students and migrants, lives tightly packed together, mostly in tenement blocks built before the end the 19th century and each with three or four courtyards. One third of the population of Kreuzberg is from overseas, mainly from Turkey, a fact which has earned the district the name 'Little Istanbul'. Kreuzberg is 'the largest Turkish city outside Turkey' and the U-Bahn to Kreuzberg is referred to as the 'Orient Express'.

Fortunately the buildings of Kreuzberg have avoided wholesale demolition. Instead, the rehabilitation of the old buildings has begun, such as the magnificent stucco facades on Planufer along the Landwehrkanal. The Riehmers Hofgarten housing complex built between 1881 and 1892, which contrasts with the ubiquitous tenement blocks, has been restored, as have the facades on Chamissoplatz. Some interesting new buildings have also been built on Fraenkelufer and at Schlesisches Tor. Despite its problems, Kreuzberg is a lively district which displays a charm all of its own, with its highly individual bars and cafés and streets full of life.

Kreuzberg has played a unique role in the artistic life of Berlin, being a place where many new movements have had their roots, especially recent developments in avant-

Chamissoplatz:
a new lease of life

49

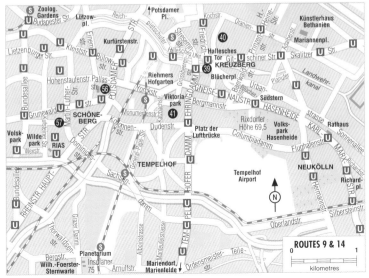

Martin Gropius Bau

Amerika Gedenkbibliothek

The Berlin Museum

Schinkel's Memorial

garde and alternative culture. Its reputation has been underpinned by the **Künstlerhaus Bethanien**, the former Bethanien Hospital on Mariannenplatz, which hosts theatre, concerts and exhibitions. The Martin-Gropius-Bau at Stresemannstrasse 10 ranks highly as a venue for changing exhibitions. Nearby, on the former Prinz Albrecht site, which was the headquarters of the SS, SD and Gestapo in 1933, is the documentary exhibition, **Topographie des Terrors** (Topography of Terror).

All that remains of the former Anhalter Bahnhof on Askanischer Platz is the restored monumental portico, the former station area being used for exhibitions. The Deutschlandhaus (Stresemannstrasse 90) has sought to encourage eastern German art and culture and the partly rebuilt Hamburger Bahnhof in Invalidenstrasse, Tiergarten, is also used for exhibitions of contemporary art.

Kreuzberg is best reached by U-Bahn Line 1 from Zoo station to Hallesches Tor. This station is on Mehringplatz (formerly Belle-Alliance-Platz) which, with Blücherplatz to the south, is the district's busiest point. Streets radiating northwards from here ended at the Wall and are still derelict; they include Friedrichstrasse and the memorial at Checkpoint Charlie, which was once the crossing point for foreign visitors to East Berlin.

On Blücherplatz is the **Amerika Gedenkbibliothek ㊴** Berlin's biggest public library, which contains almost 1 million volumes and includes a vast section on the history of Berlin. The library was built in 1954 from American donations. South of the library is the **Friedhöfe vor dem Halleschen Tor**, a cemetery which contains the graves of, among others, the poets Adelbert von Chamisso (d 1838) and E T A Hoffmann (d 1822), and the composer Felix Mendelssohn Bartholdy (d 1847). To the north, in Lindenstrasse the ★ **Berlin Museum ㊵** has found a worthy home in the baroque building of the Altes Kammergericht (Supreme Court). Its collections illustrate the development of the city from the time of the Great Elector to the 20th century. The main points of interest are the portrait gallery of Berlin's leading personalities, the Chodowiecki Kabinett, views of Berlin, documentation of Berlin humour and a toy collection. Next door, is the **Judisches Museum** (Jewish Museum), which was erected in 1998 by the architect Daniel Libeskind. It is connected with the Berlin Museum by an underground tunnel.

From Blücherplatz, Mehringdamm runs south to Platz der Luftbrücke (*see page 65*) but first turn right into Kreuzbergstrasse to find the **Kreuzberg ㊶**, the 66-m (220-ft) hill that gives the area its name. It is crowned by Schinkel's Memorial of the War of Liberation (1821). The 13-ha (36-acre) Viktoriapark with its artificial waterfall is laid out on the hillside.

Route 10

Theodor-Heuss-Platz – Messegelände (Exhibition Centre) – ★ Olympic Stadium – Spandau

This tour is really intended for motorists, but it is possible to get to Spandau by a BVG bus. The starting point is the busy **Theodor-Heuss-Platz**. In the middle of the square is a bowl where a flame used to burn; the flame was lit by Theodor Heuss and was set to burn until Germany was reunited. On 3 October 1990, the flame was extinguished. On the southern side of the square is the television tower for Sender Freies Berlin (SFB), one of Berlin's state-run television studios. The adjacent building in Masurenallee is Haus des Rundfunks or Radio House (1931).

The Messegelände

To the south of the Masurenallee is the **Messegelände** (Exhibition and Trade Fair Centre). Twenty-seven halls are linked together creating a covered area of 100,000sq m (1 million sq ft) and an open area of 40,000sq m (430,000sq ft). A number of important trade fairs are held here every year, including the Grüne Woche (Green Week) in January and February, the International Tourist Convention in March, and in October, the International Fashion Fair. At the heart of the centre is an oval garden and the **Palais am Funkturm** restaurant. The Exhibition Centre is connected by a bridge link to the International Congress Centre (ICC), opened in 1979.

51

Towering above the Exhibition Centre is the **Funkturm (Radio Tower)** 42. The 138-m (400-ft) Funkturm was built between 1924 and 1926 for the Third German Radio Exhibition and is now one of Berlin's major landmarks. A restaurant is located on the first platform at a height of 55m (160ft). The second platform at 126m (375ft) is accessible by lift and provides a ★ splendid view over Berlin (open daily 10am–11pm). At the foot of the tower

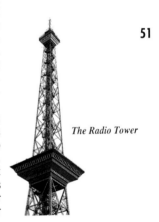

The Radio Tower

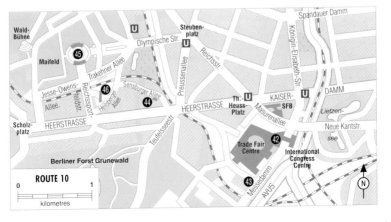

with the entrance in Messedamm is the Deutsche Rundfunkmuseum (German Radio Museum).

To the south of the Exhibition Centre is the **Deutschlandhalle 43**, which was built in 1935. It was badly damaged during the war and has been rebuilt. It can accommodate major sporting events and shows with room for 12,000 spectators. The Deutschlandhalle also marks the starting point for the **Avus**, which stands for Automobil-Verkehrs- und Übungsstrasse (motor traffic and practice track), Berlin's famous motor racing track. There are two 10-km (7-mile) straight stretches which cross the Grunewald and end in Nikolassee.

Take the Reichsstrasse exit to the northwest of Theodor-Heuss-Platz and then a left turn at Steubenplatz into Olympische Strasse which leads to the Olympic Stadium. An alternative route is to proceed west along Heerstrasse and then take a right turn into Sensburger Allee. At number 25 is the **Georg-Kolbe-Museum 44** (*see page 82*). The sculptor Georg Kolbe (1877–1947) lived and worked here. In a nearby park, the Georg-Kolbe-Hain, five of Kolbe's bronze statues are on permanent display: *Die Kniende* (Kneeling Woman), *Die Grosse Liegende* (Large Reclining Woman), *Der Stürzende* (The Falling Man), *Dionysos* and *Mars und Venus*.

Continue along Sensburger and Heilsberger Allee to reach Olympischer Platz. Werner March (1894–1976) built the ★ **Olympic Stadium 45** (daily 8am–dusk) for the XI Olympiad in 1936, on the site of a former national sports arena. The oval stadium is 300m (900ft) long and 230m (700ft) wide and can accommodate up to 80,000 spectators. There are also facilities for swimming, hockey, tennis and equestrian events. The Marathon Gate opens on to the Maifeld, an open area with space for 500,000 people. The 77-m (220-ft) tower on the western side of the stadium was rebuilt in 1962 and was equipped with a new bell weighing 4,500kg (9,918lbs). The broken bell can be seen at the stadium's southern entrance. Take the lift to the top of the tower for a fine view over Berlin.

To the south of the Olympic Stadium, at Heilsberger-Dreieck is the 17-storey **Corbusier House 46**. This building was the French architect Le Corbusier's (1887–1965) contribution to the 1957 international architectural exhibition. The block consists of 527 flats housing 1,400 residents. Corbusier called it a *unité d'habitation* (living unit) and it is a small town in its own right.

From this point it is easy to continue the tour (by bus if necessary) to the western district of Spandau via Heerstrasse and Pichelsdorfer Strasse. The road passes behind the Scholzplatz, a British cemetery, and then a bridge crosses the Stössensee. Take a left turn 300m (325yd) further on to the wooded Pichelswerder peninsula (a protected

Show of strength at the Olympic Stadium

The Corbusier House

area). Just before the Freybrücke, which crosses the Havel, take a fork to the right to the pretty fishing village of Tiefwerder. Tiefwerder is sometimes referred to as 'Little Venice on the Havel'. Behind the bridge on the right is Grimnitzsee and on the left of Heerstrasse is the village of Pichelsdorf. The latter borders the Havel bay known as Scharfe Lanke and is a popular centre for water sports enthusiasts. The Pichelsdorfer Strasse branches off to the right and leads into the centre of Spandau.

Spandau is situated at the point where the Spree and Havel merge. Strictly speaking it is older than Berlin, receiving its town charter in 1232 and retaining its independence until 1920, but nevertheless if Spandau locals need to go 'into town' then they go to Berlin. The 14th-century old town of Spandau has managed to preserve its history better than all the other districts of west Berlin; in fact it is the only genuine Berlin-style old town left.

One of the prettiest parts of the old town is the restored Kolk and the remaining section of the town wall. But despite the town's historic past, it is one of Berlin's biggest industrial areas with Siemensstadt at the heart. In the northwest corner of Berlin is the huge Spandauer Stadtforst (forest). Some parts of the forest are protected areas on account of the abundant and sometimes rare flora. The 20-ha (50-acre) Teufelsbruch is a protected area (the second biggest in Berlin after the Pfaueninsel), as are the Grosser and Kleiner Rohrpfuhl marshes.

In Reformationsplatz in Spandau's old town is the **Niko-laikirche** ⓐ. This 15th-century church is the last of Berlin's maintained churches in the bricked Gothic style typical of Brandenburg. In the restored ★ interior the 1398 bronze font and the painted limestone altar (1582), which was donated by Graf Rochus zu Lynar, are of particular interest. On the north wall of the aisle is a Gothic crucifixion scene dating from 1540. In front of the church stands a monument to the Elector Joachim II (1889) by Encke and a memorial stone designed by Schinkel in 1816 which commemorates the German Wars of Liberation between 1813 and 1815.

On the left bank of the Havel, 500m (550yd) to the north, is the **Spandau Citadel** ⓑ. This fortification, which is entirely surrounded by water, was started in 1560 based on the designs of Italian architect De Gandino. It was modelled on the new Italian defensive system of angular bastions. The gatehouse and the so-called *König* and *Königin* (king and queen) bastions were the Italian's work but, in 1578, Graf Rochus zu Lynar completed the

Spandau Citadel entrance

53

Nikolaikirche, portal detail

ROUTE 10
(continued)
0   300
metres

Citadel: the Julius Tower

construction work on the *Kronprinz* (crown prince) and *Brandenburg* bastions. The huge walls surround not only the remains of Spandauburg (c 1520) but the 32-m (90-ft) **Juliusturm** (Julius Tower) which dates from the middle of the 13th century. Also from this period is the adjacent Palais, the Gothic living quarters, main hall and the impressive burg itself. The interior of the Gothic hall was restored in 1981 and the Juliusturm was used for many years as a prison. After the Franco-Prussian war of 1870–1, the gold treasures which had been confiscated from the French as reparations were stored here. The citadel houses a local history museum and restaurant.

The two old fishing villages of Gatow and Kladow are situated within Spandau's boundary and have become popular destinations for daytrippers. The Kladowerdamm runs from Gatow to Kladow, which is now a wealthy suburb. There are also a number of attractive beer gardens on Imchenallee on the banks of the Havel. The ferries and pleasure boats which ply the waters of west Berlin call in here and there are also some popular bathing beaches in the vicinity. The island of Imchen is a bird reserve and lies just off-shore. For a pleasant walk, take Ritterfelddamm to Gross-Glienicke, a settlement on the eastern bank of the Gross-Glienicke lake. Until 3 October 1990, the border with East Germany split this lake in half.

Motorists may choose to follow the old border for the return journey. From Kladow take a northwesterly route via Ritterfelddamm and past the British air base at Gatow, on to the old farmstead at Ritterfeld and then turn right on to the Potsdamer Chaussee. This eventually becomes Wilhelmstrasse. It was here that the Nazi war criminals were brought after the Nuremberg trials of 1946. In 1987, on the death of the last prisoner, Hitler's deputy Rudolf Hess, the prison was demolished.

Ranged artillery in the Citadel

Route 11

Through the ★ Grunewald to the Wannsee

The Grunewald can be reached by U-Bahn, bus or car. Leave Zoo station via Hardenbergstrasse, Ernst-Reuter-Platz, Bismarckstrasse, Kaiserdamm and Heerstrasse. Turn left at Scholzplatz into Am Postfenn which then skirts round the northern tip of the Grunewald to the Havel. The beaches along the 10-km (7-mile) Havelchaussee have become the territory of Berlin water sports enthusiasts.

Sailing boats on the Havel

The ★ **Grunewald**, the 40-sqkm (15-sq mile) forest which links the districts of Wilmersdorf and Zehlendorf, starts just south of Heerstrasse and extends 9km (6 miles) south as far as the Wannsee, one of Berlin's main lakes. On its western edge it is bordered by the ★ Havelchaussee with its many bays and beaches. To the east and south are several smaller lakes such as the Schlachtensee and Krumme Lanke in the Zehlendorf village of Nikolassee. These lakes can be reached by taking the underground to Krumme Lanke U-Bahn station and then crossing Argentinische Allee into Fischerhüttenstrasse; there is also an S-Bahn connection to Schlachtensee.

Both lakes have a number of small bathing beaches and one of the attractions of the Schlachtensee is the **Alte Fischerhütte**, a café and beer garden which also has rowing boats for hire. A walk round the two lakes could also be combined with a visit to the **Haus am Waldsee** (Argentinische Allee 30), an art gallery which displays the work of modern artists.

It is only a few minutes drive from here to **Düppel Museumsdorf** (Museum Village) in Zehlendorf-Süd (Clauertstrasse 11), where a medieval settlement (c 1200–20) has been recreated on Machnower Fenn. This provides the setting for demonstrations of medieval weaving, pottery and construction techniques. The museum village is situated on the edge of the Düppel forest, between Nikolassee, Wannsee and the old, southwestern border with the GDR, and it is one of four huge forested areas within the confines of the Berlin conurbation. Düppeler forest is probably the quietest of the four and, even in summer, few people venture into the more remote areas of these peaceful woods.

During World War II, over 40 percent of the timber in the Grunewald was felled, but about 24 million trees have since been planted and 6 million of these are deciduous ones, which have managed to relieve the gloom of what is otherwise mainly pine forest. Some marshland and a few small lakes have been designated as nature reserves and the area is home to red deer, fallow deer, wild boar and small game birds. Near the Teufelssee on Teufelssee-

A haven for wildlife

chaussee is the 115-m (350-ft) **Teufelsberg**, an artificial hill created from wartime rubble which is now managed woodland. It has become Berlin's winter sports centre with a toboggan run, two ski jumps, a ski lift and a snow cannon to make artificial snow. Teufelssee and Teufelsfenn have been nature reserves since 1960.

Souvenirs at the Grunewaldturm

Take the road Am Postfenn off Scholzplatz to the Havel and follow the **Havelchaussee** south. On the other side of the bay known as Jürgenlanke is the Schildhorn peninsula. At the top of a small mound, a sandstone column with a cross and inscription marks the spot where the last Wendish prince, Jaczo, swam across the Havel to safety with his horse when pursued by Albrecht the Bear. He put his escape down to divine intervention and immediately became a follower of Christ.

A road leads off Havelchaussee round the Dachsberg (61m/180ft), continues along the side of the lake to the Karlsberg (79m/240ft) and then passes the 56-m (170-ft) **Grunewaldturm** ㊾. Constructed in 1898 from red bricks in the traditional Brandenburg style, this tower was originally built in memory of Kaiser William I, and was called the Kaiser-Wilhelm-Turm. There is a splendid view as far as Potsdam and Berlin city centre from the top of tower, which stands 135m (400ft) above the Havel. A 15-minute walk away from the tower is the **Forsthaus Saubucht**, a wild boar reserve. The Grunewaldturm restaurant is a popular haunt.

The ferry crosses to Lindwerder

The Havelchaussee returns to the shores of the Havel at Lieper Bucht and only a short distance further on a ferry crosses to the pretty island of Lindwerder. The main road continues south as far as the bay at Grosse Steinlanke but then bears left, cuts through the woods and becomes Kronprinzessinnenweg as it runs parallel to the Avus (*see page 52*) and then leads into Nikolassee and the **Wannsee**.

Take a right turn into Wannseebadweg just before Nikolassee for the **Wannsee bathing beach** ㊿. The Lido, which is Berlin's biggest open-air swimming pool, was opened in 1907. On hot summer days it is not unusual for over 30,000 people to head for the beach which extends for 1300m (about 1 mile) and is 80m (250ft) wide. After an afternoon sunbathing and swimming, it is pleasant to sit on the terrace at the thatched **Wannsee-Terrassen restaurant** and absorb the atmosphere. The island of Schwanenwerder is connected to the mainland by a causeway and has been inhabited since 1882. The island is now home to the world famous **Aspen Institute for Humanistic Studies** with Schwanenwerder as the only centre for the foundation outside the USA. Just before the causeway on the mainland side, a footpath branches off to the right and leads to the Grosses Fenster, from where the view extends northwards up the Havel as far as Spandau.

Wannsee bathing beach

Route 12

Around the Grunewaldsee

This route begins on the Kurfürstendamm where the No 119 (or No 129) bus to Roseneck starts. From Roseneck, follow Clayallee (with the Grunewald on the right-hand side) as far as Pücklerstrasse or alternatively take the No 115 bus to Pücklerstrasse. To visit the Grunewald hunting lodge or the lake, get off the bus at the Königin-Luise-Strasse stop. This road leads directly to the hunting lodge and the lake.

The ★ **Brücke Museum** ❺❶ in Bussardsteig (*see page 82*) was opened in 1967 at the instigation of the painter

Brücke Museum

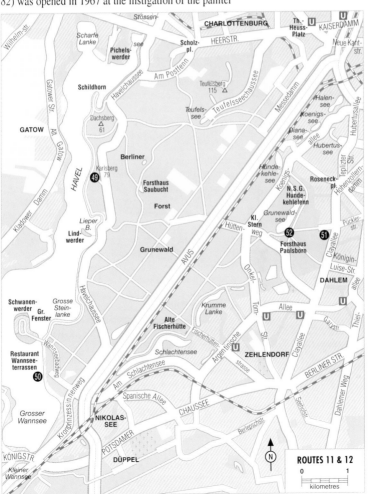

Girl's Head by Kirchner, 1930

Jagdschloss Grunewald

An outing to Grunewald Lake

Karl Schmidt-Rotluff, to whom the museum is dedicated, presented a large part of his work to the museum. Schmidt-Rotluff was one of the German Expressionists who founded the famous artists' group known as *Die Brücke* (The Bridge) in Dresden in 1905. The group later settled in Berlin.

Most of the exhibits are by either Schmidt-Rotluff or Erich Heckel but other painters from the group, including Ernst-Ludwig Kirchner, Max Pechstein and Otto Mueller have work exhibited here, as do Max Kaus, Emy Röder, Otto Herbig and Emil Nolde, who were at some time associated with the Expressionists.

A footpath leads down to the Grunewaldsee and the ★ **Jagdschloss Grunewald** (Grunewald Hunting Lodge) 🔄 which is situated on the bank of the lake (summer Tuesday to Sunday 10am–1pm, 1.30–4pm). This Renaissance-style lodge was built in 1542 by Caspar Theyss for the Elector Joachim III. In 1593, the architect Graf Rochus zu Lynar built some farm buildings and the stables. More farm buildings were added in 1770 by Frederick the Great. The furnishings date from the time of King Frederick I, but Frederick William II and Frederick William III often used the hunting lodge as a retreat.

The cosy ground-floor rooms are in the hunting tradition: beautiful baroque furniture, tasteful Berlin porcelain, hunting trophies, animal and hunting pictures from the 17th and 18th century. On the first floor, a remarkable collection of paintings by German and Dutch masters (15th–19th century) has been assembled, including works by Blomaert, Bruyn, Bol, Jordaens and Rubens, Cranach the Elder and Graff. More paintings from the time of Frederick the Great and the Berlin Biedermeier period complete the collection. In one of the outlying buildings, there is a small hunting museum and in the summer months, occasional concerts are held in the courtyard.

After the hunting lodge, either turn right to the **Forsthaus Paulsborn**, a forester's lodge built 160 years ago and now a hotel and restaurants or turn left towards Clayallee and the Chalet Suisse. Alternatively, take a stroll along the bank of the Grunewald lake, typical of the Brandenburg region, and through the adjacent conservation area of Hundekehlefenn and northwards into the wealthy Grunewald suburb around the Koenigsallee, which links the Grunewald with the Kurfürstendamm. To the left of Koenigsallee are the Dianasee and the Koenigssee and to the right the Hertasee and the Hubertussee; on the junction with Wallotstrasse is a memorial to Walther Rathenau, a foreign minister who was assassinated there on 24 June 1922. To get back to Zoo station, head for the western end of the Kurfürstendamm which begins just beyond the Halensee.

Route 13

Free University – ★★ Dahlem Museums – ★ Botanical Gardens

This route begins at U-Bahn Oskar Helene Heim (by the university hospital of the same name) and leads through the Dahlem university campus to the Dahlem Museum and Botanical Garden.

The **Freie Universität (Free University)** 🔢 was founded on 4 December 1948 after the division of Berlin. The first rector of the Free University or FU was the historian Friedrich Meinecke who died in 1954. Between 1950 and 1954, the modern main building, the Henry Ford Building, with the Auditorium Maximum and Library, were built with funds from the Henry Ford Foundation. Numerous new buildings followed, but even today a large number of university departments are housed in villas in the quiet streets of Dahlem.

The university is bursting at the seams. In 1992, there were 62,000 students – when it opened its doors in 1948 there were only 1,500! With 146,000 students attending the Free University, Humboldt University, Technical College and College of the Arts, Berlin has a greater claim than Munich to be Germany's biggest academic centre. A restructuring of the Technical College and Free University departments with those of Humboldt University is under way.

Follow the U-Bahn, which runs at street level here, to reach Königin-Luise-Strasse. With Dahlem's village green, the half-timbered Dahlem-Dorf U-Bahn station and the medieval Annenkirche (14th–15th century), give an insight into how the old tied village of **Dahlem** used to look. Among the graves in the churchyard are those of the historian Friedrich Meinecke (1862–1954), the sculptor of animal figures August Gaul (1869–1921) and several famous actors.

Freie Universität

59

Dahlem-Dorf U-Bahn Station

ROUTE 13
0   500
metres

Picture Gallery: Titian's Venus with Cupid and the Organ Player

★★ Dahlem Museums ⑤

Arnimallee 23–7 and Lansstrasse 8. U-Bahn Dahlem-Dorf and buses Nos 110, 180 (*see page 82* for opening times).

Berlin's world-famous museums shared the fate of the divided city. Today they are concentrated at four locations: Schloss Charlottenburg, Dahlem, Kulturforum, south of the Tiergarten in the west, and also at their former focal point of Museumsinsel in east Berlin. When in 1953 the art treasures were returned to Berlin from their wartime homes in bunkers and mineworkings, those stored in central Germany found their way to east Berlin, while those from western Germany went to west Berlin, where new homes for them had to be found.

For a long time, the resulting Dahlem Museum has been the most important museum in the western part of the city, but now, after reunification of the east and west collections, the painting gallery is being moved to its own building in the Kulturforum and the sculpture gallery has moved to the Bode Museum on the Museum Island. Visitors should note that the entire Dahlem museum is due to close until the end of the year 2000, while its collection undergoes total reorganisation. However, since the artworks in the collection are of such international importance, details on them are still given below, in preparation for the reopening of the new galleries towards the end of 2000.

The Dahlem museum has in its collections items from the state collections of the Stiftung Preussischer Kulturbesitz (Foundation for Prussian Cultural Heritage) in the ★ Museum of Anthropology, and the Museum for East Asian and Indian Art. The main entrance to the original museum is in Arnimallee.

The paintings in the ★★★ **Gemäldegalerie** (Picture Gallery) give a magnificent overview of all periods of Eu-

Playful distractions at Dahlem

ropean painting from the 13th to the 18th century. The main emphasis is on internationally acclaimed German, Italian and Dutch paintings. After the war, the original collection of paintings had to be dispersed – some were held in Dahlem, others in the Picture Gallery on the Museumsinsel. New book collections have now been reunited at the Kulturforum.

There are excellent examples of 14th- and 15th-century Italian painting with masterpieces by ★ Botticelli, Fra Filippo Lippi, Caravaggio, Verrocchio and others. The five Madonnas by ★★ Rafaello are a major highlight. Work by ★ Mantegna, Bellini, Giorgione and ★ Titian (*Venus with Cupid and the Organ Player, Self-Portrait*) represent the painting of northern Italy. The 18th-century Venetian school is represented above all by Tiepolo and Canaletto, many of whose famous ★★ views of Venice can be seen here. The Italian collection is arguably the most important one outside Italy.

The Dutch section is of similar high standing. The gallery's 21 pictures by ★ Rembrandt (including ★ *Portrait of Hendrickje Stoffels*, two self-portraits and portraits of his wife Saskia) form the world's second largest Rembrandt collection. Since 1985, it has been established that the world famous ★ *Man with a Golden Helmet* is not an original Rembrandt, but was painted instead by one of the so-called 'Rembrandt circle'.

There are further celebrated works by Jan van Eyck, Peter Brueghel the Elder (★ *Dutch Proverbs*), Hugo van der Goes, Frans Hals (★ *Malle Babbe*), Terborch (★ *The Concert*) and Vermeer (★ *Woman with Pearl Necklace*). The museum also has in its collection a number of pictures by Rubens.

Of special interest in the German section are works by Albrecht Dürer (★ *Portrait of Hieronymus Holzschuher*, and others), Albrecht Altdorfer (★ *Rest on the Flight into Egypt, Birth of Christ*), Martin Schongauer (★ *Adoration of the Shepherds*) and Lucas Cranach the Elder (*The Fount of Youth*). Hans Holbein the Younger's ★★ *Portrait of the Merchant Georg Gisze* is also much admired.

Holbein's Portrait of the Merchant Georg Gisze

French masters of the 17th and 18th century are represented by Nicolas Poussin, Claude Lorrain, ★★ Watteau (*French Comedy, Italian Comedy*), Pesne and others. From the Spanish school come El Greco (★★ *Mater Dolorosa*), Goya and Velasquez to name but a few.

The **Museum für Indische Kunst (Museum of Indian Art)** was established in 1963 and is the youngest of all the state museums in Berlin. It houses Germany's most important collection of Indian art. The institute owns approximately 15,000 objects, and nearly 600 bronzes, stone sculptures, wood carvings, paintings and textiles from India, Pakistan and neighbouring countries are on show to visitors on the first floor.

Skulpturenabteilung: discus thrower by Schadow

The collection is divided up into three parts: India, South-east Asia and Central Asia. Visitors can see exquisite exhibits of the three main regions, among them a large textile picture, woven by Krishna admirers, and a wooden house-temple from West India, which measures 2.4-m (7¾-ft) high and is still in very good condition. Of particular note are the Turfansammlung (named after the oasis of Turfan in eastern Turkestan), a valuable collection of unique frescoes from circa 500 BC to AD 900, depicting the life of Buddha, and the Gandhara collection, which features major Buddhist stone reliefs and sculptures dating from the 1st century.

Museum für Indische Kunst: Buddha and Indian doll

The **Museum für Ostasiatische Kunst (Museum of East Asian Art)** displays Chinese, Mongolian, Korean and Japanese art from 1700 BC to the present day and features bronzes, painting, ceramics, textiles. The museum was founded by the art historian Wilhelm von Bode (1845–1919), who was a friend of the German emperor Wilhelm II whom he persuaded to donate money. Nearly 90 percent of the collection was carried by the Red Army to the Hermitage at St Petersburg in 1945, where it still resides today. However, 300 objects remained behind in Berlin, and this collection has been added to by purchases over the past 50 years.

The ★★ **Museum für Völkerkunde (Museum of Anthropology)** is one of the leading museums of its kind in Europe. The collection on which the museum was originally based was established as long ago as the 17th century by Friedrich Wilhelm, the Great Elector.

Today, with its enormous variety of sculptures, paintings, cult objects and masks, and everyday items such as clothes, tools and household utensils, the Museum of Anthropology is a veritable eldorado for all those interested in other cultures.

Museum für Volkerkunde: crafts from exotic lands

There are sections covering Africa (including some notable bronzes from Benin and a selection of West African masks), the South Seas (covering Hawaii, Polynesia, Micronesia and atoll cultures) the Americas (including South American jungle Indians, Peru, Ecuador, Chile, northwest Argentina, Mexico, Mayan region) as well as Southern Asia and East Asia.

Of particular interest is the Gold Room which displays items of jewellery from Peru, including some that are approximately 3,000 years old, while the South Seas section contains reconstructions of dwellings from New Zealand and New Guinea. There is also a special section devoted exclusively to ethnic music, which has in its collection some 60,000 recordings. The highlight of the museum, however – particularly for children – is the Boat Hall, where the captivating exhibits include an impressive double-keel craft from the Tonga Islands.

Close by, at Im Winkel 6, is the **Museum für Deutsche Volkskunde (Museum of German Folklore)**, which was originally founded in 1889 by a private collector and transferred to the state museums at the beginning of the 20th century. On display here are collections of furniture, tools, costume, textiles, etc from the German-speaking world dating from the 17th–19th centuries.

Archivstrasse 12 is home to the **Geheime Staatsarchiv**, a collection of documents recounting the history of the German nation and the eastern provinces of Prussia during the period of the Holy Roman Empire, a library and family documents.

On Königin-Luise-Strasse towards Steglitz is one entrance to the ★ **Botanical Gardens** ⓹ (daily, summer 9am–7 or 8pm, winter 9am–4 or 5pm; admission charge). Another entrance is in Unter den Eichen, south of Hermann-Ehlers-Platz. The 42-ha (100-acre) grounds are attractively laid out with the Victoria Regia House and the 25-m (80-ft) high Palm House deserving a special mention. The Gardens are very highly recommended for both sunny and rainy days. If it rains, visitors can take shelter for hours in the hothouses, one of which – the palatial glass **Tropenhaus** (the tropical hothouse) – is the largest hothouse in the world.

Stepping Stones in the Botanical Gardens

63

A large part of the garden (known as the *Freigelände*) is taken up by the extensive geographical section, where flora from the Pyrenees, the Alps, the Carpathians, the Balkans, the Caucasus and the Himalayas are on show. Attractively laid-out paths wind their way though the different temperate zones. In all, the gardens contain approximately 18,000 different species of trees and plants.

The **Botanical Museum** (opening times as for the Botanical Gardens), situated by the entrance on Königin-Luise-Platz, is the only one of its kind in Germany. Its library, which contains more than 60,000 volumes, is a fine research archive for botanists.

The Botanical Gardens

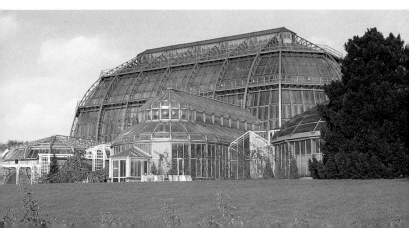

Exterior décor at the Planetarium

Route 14

Schöneberg – Tempelhof – Neukölln
Please refer to the map on page 49

Potsdamer Strasse amusements

Take the U-Bahn from Zoo station to U-Bahn Kurfürstenstrasse in **Schöneberg.** The U-Bahn is located on dreary Potsdamer Strasse, a street of entertainment to satisfy the lowest common denominator, with cheap bars, hotels, sex shows and amusement arcades. It leads northwards to the Nationalgalerie, Philharmonie and Potsdamer Platz (*see page 18*) where Schöneberg borders on the districts of Tiergarten and Mitte. To the south it runs through the centre of Schöneberg, becoming Hauptstrasse, then Rheinstrasse and finally ending in Friedenau, still a relatively quiet area with a lot of architecture from the *Gründerzeit*, the boom years towards the end of the last century.

In the south of Schöneberg, where it borders on Steglitz, is the impressive observatory, the **Wilhelm-Foerster-Sternwarte**, situated on top of the Insulaner, a 75-m (230-ft) mound of wartime rubble. It is a regular meeting place for amateur astronomers and the public are invited to join in the sessions (Tuesday, Thursday–Saturday until 9pm, Sunday at 3, 4, 6 and 9pm). At the bottom of the hill, in the Planetarium by the Insulaner open-air pool, there are regular public lectures and exhibitions.

Further south from the U-Bahn on the right along Potsdamer Strasse is the **Kleistpark** ㊱, which began life in 1679 as the Great Elector's vegetable garden and for many years formed the main part of the Botanical Gardens until it moved to Dahlem in 1900 (*see page 60*). The King's Colonnades, designed by Gontard between 1777 and 1780 and brought here from Alexanderplatz in 1910, form the entrance to the park.

The **Altes Kammergericht** (Supreme Court) in the park is where the notorious *Volksgerichtshof* (People's Court) show trials of the Third Reich took place. Between 1945 and 1948, the Allied Control Council met here. In 1954, it was host to the Foreign Ministers' Conference and in 1971 the Four Powers' Agreement was signed. But it was another 18 years before the four allies' ambassadors met here on 11 December 1989 to discuss the latest political events. In 1991 the Supreme Court returned to the impressive building of 1913.

Take a right turn off Potsdamer Strasse into Grunewald-strasse and then left into Martin-Luther-Strasse to reach John-F-Kennedy-Platz. Here is **Schöneberg Town Hall** ❺. This building, erected between 1911 and 1914, was the office of the mayor of Berlin until 1991, when he returned to his traditional home in the Rotes Rathaus (Red Town Hall) in the east. Until April 1993, it hosted the sittings of the Berlin Chamber of Deputies, which now meets in the old Prussian Assembly building in Niederkirchner Strasse on the border between Tiergarten and Berlin-Mitte, which was in noman's land until 1989. Every day at noon, the Liberty Bell – a copy of the Liberty Bell in Philadelphia, presented to the people of Berlin in 1950 by General Clay in the name of the 17 million Americans who donated money – rings out from the 70-m (230-ft) high tower. The inscription reads 'May this world, with God's help, see a rebirth of freedom'.

Detail: Schöneberg Town Hall

A bronze plaque on the town hall entrance commemorates the visit by John F Kennedy on 26 June 1963, and his now famous speech from the balcony to the people of Berlin in which he uttered those stirring, immortal words, '*Ich bin ein Berliner*'.

From Schöneberg town hall, **Tempelhof** is best reached via Dominicusstrasse, Hauptstrasse, Kolonnenstrasse and Dudenstrasse, ending at Platz der Luftbrücke, behind which is the main entrance to Tempelhof Airport.

Since 1951, the 20-m (66-ft) ★ Airlift Memorial, by Eduard Ludwig has stood in front of the Tempelhof airport buildings. The Berliners call it Hungerkralle (The Claws of Hunger). Its three arcs stretching westwards symbolise the Allied relief flights through the air corridor to Tempelhof, Tegel and Gatow airports during the 11-month blockade of 1948 and 1949.

Zentralflughafen Tempelhof (Tempelhof Central Airport) occupies most of Tempelhofer Feld which, in Imperial days, was a parade ground. In 1908, the Wright Brothers demonstrated their first powered aircraft here. The early days of German commercial aviation are associated with this site and in 1926 Deutsche Lufthansa was founded. The current airport building was built between 1934 and 1939. In 1975, it was closed to civilian flights when Tegel airport opened but it is now in use for passenger traffic once again.

In Mariendorfer Damm in Mariendorf is west Berlin's only trotting track. On the corner of Mariendorfer Damm and Alt Mariendorf is the medieval church of Mariendorf, a 13th-century structure built from local stone. Dating from 1220 it is Berlin's oldest village church, and it stands on the village green in ★★ **Marienfelde**. From Platz der Luftbrücke, Columbiadamm and Flughafenstrasse lead to the district of **Neukölln**.

The ★★ **Volkspark Hasenheide**, at one time a hunting ground belonging to the Great Elector, lies between Columbiadamm and Hasenheide. A memorial marks the spot where the German nationalist and 'Father of Gymnastics' Ludwig Jahn, inaugurated the first public gymnastics area in 1811.

Ludwig Jahn memorial

Flughafenstrasse leads on to Neukölln town hall (1908) on Karl-Marx-Strasse. To the southwest, a village **blacksmith's shop** still operates on Richardplatz, the Rixdorf village green. Between Richardstrasse and Kirchgasse can be found the remains of the former Böhmische Dorf (Bohemian Village), where in 1737, a colony of Bohemians made their new home, safe from religious persecution. On the corner of Richardstrasse and Kirchgasse the 'grateful descendants of the Bohemians welcomed in this place' erected a monument to Frederick William I, King of Prussia. Like his son and successor Frederick II, he frequently offered asylum to political or religious refugees. Today the old working-class areas of Neukölln have a high proportion of foreign *Gastarbeiter* (guest workers). In the south of Neukölln, on the site of the 1985 Bundesgartenschau (German Garden Show), is the 90-ha (220-acre) **Britzer Garten** with 22km (14 miles) of footpaths and a lakeside restaurant.

The blacksmith's shop on Richardplatz

Route 15

Through Wedding and Reinickendorf

This route takes in the former French sector, which comprised the districts of Wedding and Reinickendorf. The areas of greatest interest are the Tegeler See with Humboldt Castle and Tegeler Forst (forest). The quickest way to get there using public transport is on the U-Bahn Line 9 (Rathaus Steglitz – Zoo – Osloer Strasse) which connects with Line 6 (Alt Mariendorf – Tegel) at Leopoldplatz.

By car, the best way is to head northeast from Ernst-Reuter-Platz (*see page 37*), via Marchstrasse and Franklinstrasse. This leads through Moabit in the Tiergarten district, the hub of Berlin's judicial system, with the Criminal Court and Remand Centre in Turmstrasse. After crossing the Spree, take a left turn followed immediately by a right turn into Beusselstrasse. Beyond the bridge over the Westhafenkanal, the road leads right up to **Plötzensee Juvenile Prison** in the Charlottenburg district. It was here that almost 3,000 victims of Nazism, including conspirators who took part in the 20 July 1944 plot, members of the 'Red Chapel' and the 'Kreisau Circle' were executed. In the prison yard is the Plötzensee memorial, which commemorates the victims of National Socialism.

From the prison, Heckerdamm leads to an imposing building, the church of ★ **Maria Regina Martyrium** 🔢 which was built by the Würzburg architects Hans Schädel and Friedrich Ebert between 1961–2 as a memorial to victims of the National Socialist reign of terror. The simple, square building was financed by donations from Catholics from all over Germany. The church includes a parish house and a large area for the celebration of Mass with an open-air altar, a mighty block of bronze wearing a crown of thorns. The wall running along the right-hand side of the area bears the stations of the cross, which, like the altar, are the work of Herbert Hajek.

67

Maria Regina Martyrium: bronze altar and bells

As well as an altar, the crypt contains three symbolic tombs. On the left is a tomb for the cathedral dean, Bernhard Lichtenberg, the right-hand tomb bears the ashes of Erich Klausener, the leader of *Katholische Aktion*, and between them lies a tomb for the martyrs who were denied a burial or whose graves are unknown.

Return via Seestrasse to **Wedding**, a working-class area still dominated by 19th-century tenement blocks with their gloomy courtyards. It is also home to companies with worldwide reputations such as AEG, Osram, and Schering. In the 1920s, Wedding was a communist stronghold, especially around Kösliner Strasse, as poverty and factory work characterised the daily round in this proletarian quarter, but little remains of the district's working-class his-

The gloomy side of Wedding

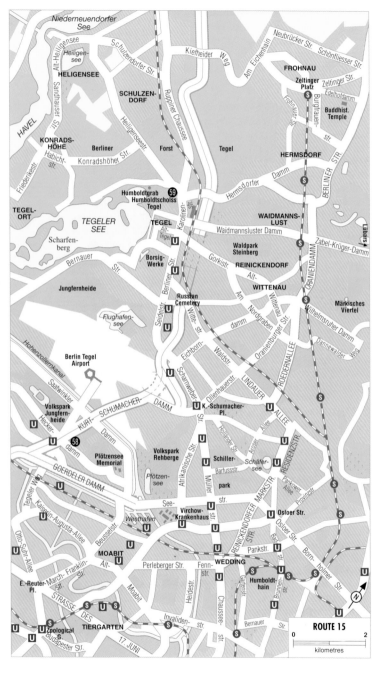

68

ROUTE 15

0   2

kilometres

tory. Much of the area has been demolished, including many old but habitable 19th-century buildings that documented the history of the district.

The streets of Wedding near what was the Berlin Wall have some sorry tales to tell. Bernauer Strasse, in particular, in the southeast of the district will always have a place in the history books. It was known as 'death strip', for it was here where buildings on one side of the street belonging to the GDR were torn down in the early days of the Wall, that many people saw no other route to freedom than to jump from their windows as the demolition teams moved in. There is now a memorial to the victims.

Bernauer Strasse has bitter memories

The painter Otto Nagel (1894–1967) is one of Wedding's famous sons. As a communist in the Nazi years he was forbidden to paint and was sentenced to imprisonment in a concentration camp.

Follow Seestrasse past West Berlin's largest hospital, the Rudolf Virchow University Clinic, then turn left into Müllerstrasse, which leads to **Reinickendorf**.

Beyond Kurt-Schumacher-Platz, Müllerstrasse becomes Scharnweberstrasse, then Seidelstrasse passing Tegel Airport, Tegel Prison, the Borsig factory and ending at Tegel U-Bahn station in Berlinerstrasse. From here it is only a few minutes through the streets of the old town to the delightful **Tegeler See** with promenade, restaurants and a large lido.

Schloss Tegel/Humboldt Museum ⑤ (May to September, Monday 10am–12am, 3pm–5pm) is at Adelheidallee 19–20. 'Humboldt's Castle' originated as the Great Elector's hunting lodge, which was converted by Schinkel between 1822–4 for Wilhelm von Humboldt. Today it is still in the hands of the Humboldt family's successors. The rooms decorated to Schinkel's design contain countless reminders of the two von Humboldt brothers – Wilhelm, the philologist and founder of the Berlin University, and Alexander, the naturalist. Furniture, antique sculptures, some of which are copies, and family portraits are on display.

Schloss Tegel houses the Humboldt Museum

In the beautiful and extensive Schlosspark, which was probably laid out by the celebrated Prussian landscape gardener Peter Joseph Lénne, an avenue of linden trees lines the route to the 'Humboldt oak' and beyond to the ★ **Humboldt family tomb**. The tomb, like Humboldt's Castle, was also designed by Schinkel. It was constructed in 1830 and in 1831 saw the addition of a copy of Thorvaldsen's *Hope*; the original *Spes* was erected here in 1993.

After a tour of the castle, a visit should be paid to the poignant but almost forgotten **Russian Cemetery** (Wittestrasse 37). The Fraternity of Saint Vladimir acquired the land in 1890 from a Wittenau farmer. In 1893, the cemetery was opened and in order to retain some links with the homeland, not just trees, but also soil was brought

The chapel at the Russian Cemetery

Russian Orthodox crosses

Lübars is over 700 years old

to Berlin from Russia. In 1894, the beautiful chapel of St Constantine and St Helen was built. Beneath the head-stones lie the remains of those who fled Tsarist Russia for Berlin. The former Russian Minister of War and General Adjutant to the Tsar, V A Suchomlinov, who died in Berlin in 1926, is also buried here. The most impressive memorial is to the Imperial Russian orchestra leader and famous composer, Mikhail Glinka (1804–57), who died in Berlin but was buried in his homeland.

From the castle, Karolinenstrasse, which becomes Ruppiner Chaussee, leads through Tegeler Forst to Schulzendorf and Heiligensee, on the old city boundary. To the south, on the peninsula between the Havel and Tegeler See, are two popular summer haunts: Konradshöhe and Tegelort.

It is worth continuing in this direction to the northernmost edge of the city either by car or by BVG bus to Hermsdorf, Frohnau, Waidmannslust and Lübars. The buses leave from Tegel U-Bahn station. Hermsdorf, founded in the 13th century, has developed into an attractive area with many country houses. Frohnau was established in 1900 by Prince Henckel von Donnersmarck as a garden suburb, and among its buildings is one of Europe's few Buddhist temples at Edelhofdamm 54. It was built between 1922–4 in east Asian style for the doctor and philologist Dr Paul Dahlke. In 1963, it was bought by the Buddhist community of Ceylon which sends monks to Berlin.

Finally, a trip to **Lübars,** a genuinely rural village over 700 years old, is recommended. It lies north of the controversial satellite town, Märkisches Viertel. Around the village green are grouped a small church dating from 1793, old farms and the cosy **Alte Dorfkrug Lübars** country café and beer garden. Lübars is the last of the Berlin villages where a farmer still makes a living from the land.

Route 16

Wannsee – ★ Pfaueninsel – Kohlhasenbrück

This route leads to the southwesterly tip of the city with its splendid landscape of woods, lakes and cultural monuments. The quickest way to the **Wannsee** by car is via the Avus (*see page 52*). From Zoo station take the S-Bahn to Wannsee, then bus No 116 or 216 to Pfaueninsel.

Wannsee: Church of St Peter and Paul

From the park above Wannsee station, there is a fine view over the **Grosse Wannsee**, a 260-ha (650-acre) arm of the Havel. To the southwest it is linked to a series of small lakes: the Kleine Wannsee, Pohlesee, Stölpchensee and Griebnitzsee. To reach the lakes, take Bismarckstrasse, a turning off Potsdamer Chaussee. At the end of the road, lying slightly to the right, is the grave of the poet Heinrich von Kleist who, on 21 November 1811, took his own life and that of his married lover, Henriette Vogel. Below the park overlooking Grosse Wannsee is the jetty for the pleasure boats to Kladow, Pfaueninsel, Nikolskoe, Glienicke Bridge, Potsdam, Caputh, Werder and other destinations.

The **Wannseevilla**, Am Grossen Wannsee 56–58 (Monday to Friday 10am–6pm; Saturday and Sunday 2pm–6pm), was opened in January 1992 as a memorial to the Holocaust. It was here, at the Wannsee Conference on 20 January 1942, that the decision was made about the 'Final Solution to the Jewish Question' – the annihilation of the Jews in occupied Europe.

71

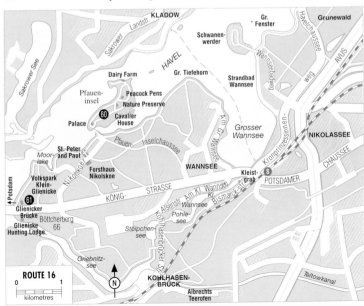

The castle

The dairy dates from 1795

Ruling the roost on Pfaueninsel

To visit Pfaueninsel by car turn right out of Kronprinzessinnenweg into Königstrasse. Just before the Volkspark Glienicke take a further right turn into Nikolskoer Weg, which leads to the landing stage. Dogs are not allowed on the Pfaueninsel and smoking is prohibited.

The ★ **Pfaueninsel (Peacock Island)** ⑩ is a nature reserve and a popular destination for day trips. It is 1.5km (about 1 mile) long and 500m (550yd) wide. The history of the island goes back to the 17th century, when it was known as Kaninchenwerder or Rabbit Island. In 1685, the Great Elector set up a laboratory for the alchemist Johann Kunckel to make gold. Instead, Kunckel succeeded in making improvements to ruby glass, a highly prized commodity at the time. 'Kunckel glass' became world-famous.

The castle (28 March to 9 May and 13 to 31 October, Saturday–Sunday 10am–5pm; 10 May to 12 October, Tuesday–Sunday, 10am–1pm, 1.30pm–5pm) on the southwest corner of the island, was built between 1794 and 1797 by the Potsdam court cabinet-maker Brendel. Reflecting the tastes of the time, it was built in the style of a ruin for Countess Lichtenau, the lifelong companion of Frederick William II. Recent work has restored it to its 1794 appearance.

Begin the tour of the island from the castle and take a look at Jakobsbrunnen (Jacob's Well), the Kavalierhaus in the middle of the island (Schinkel extended the building in 1826), the dairy at the northern end which was built at the same time as the castle in 1795, the memorial to Queen Luise, the aviaries and greenhouses.

But the real charm of the island lies in its magnificent flora, including centuries-old oaks, Californian mammoth pines, ginkgos and a cedar of Lebanon. The Pfauenhof, as its name denotes, is home to the island's peacocks. In 1894 the stream, waterfall and pond were once again laid out in their original design.

Return to the landing stage on the mainland for several other destinations, such as the **Nikolskoe** and the neighbouring church of **St Peter and St Paul**. The log cabin at Nikolskoe, now a café popular with tourists, was built in 1819 in authentic Russian style on the orders of Frederick William III for his daughter Charlotte, who later became a Russian tsarina.

The log cabin is now a café

There is a fine view over the Havel from this point. The church of St Peter and St Paul (1834–7) was also built in the Russian style. On the hour between 10am and 5pm the belltower chimes to the tune of *Üb immer Treu und Redlichkeit*, which once rang out from the tower of the Garrison Church in Potsdam. The road follows the inlet known as Moorlake, past the Volkspark Klein-Glienicke (footpath only) to the **Glienicke Bridge**, now restored as a direct link between Klein-Glienicke and Potsdam and also a BVG bus route. Until the end of 1989, it was known in East Germany as the 'Bridge of Unity' and it became famous as the place where Soviet and American secret agents were exchanged.

Greek curiosities in the grounds of Klein-Glienicke Palace

The ★ **Klein-Glienicke Palace** ❸, which was restored in 1984, lies about 100m (110yd) further on. The palace in its present form dates from 1826 and is another example of Schinkel's architectural genius. He redesigned a pleasure palace, built in 1764, to make an Italian-style summer retreat for Prince Karl, son of Queen Luise. Fragments of sculpture and architectural features brought from Italy by Prince Karl are built into the walls. The 90-ha (220-acre) romantic, ★ **Volkspark Klein-Glienicke** was laid out at the beginning of the 19th century by the landscape artist Peter Joseph Lenné (1789–1866). It contains several notable buildings including, in the southwest corner of the park, Grosse Neugierde (Large Curiosity), a circular garden pavilion with Corinthian columns, created in 1835 by Schinkel after the memorial to Lysikrates in Athens; and the teahouse Kleine Neugierde (Small Curiosity) with its antique tomb reliefs.

Some fragments are built into the walls

South of Königstrasse is the **Jagdschloss Glienicke**, a hunting lodge built in 1854 on the site of an old lodge belonging to the Great Elector (1682). In 1885, it was redesigned and the main building was again rebuilt in 1963. Today it is an adult education centre. Further on, south of Königstrasse towards Wannsee, lies the Böttcherberg, a hill which rises to a height of 66m (200ft).

From the Jagdschloss, Königstrasse leads back to Wannsee station. It is worth making a detour to see the series of lakes (*see map, page 71*) which lie to the south of Wannsee and also to **Kohlhasenbrück.** It was here, in 1540, according to the story *Michael Kohlhaas* by Heinrich von Kleist (1777–1811) that the hero of the tale ambushed a convoy carrying silver bullion.

Route 17

Köpenick – Erkner

The best way to reach Köpenick and Erkner is via the S-Bahn. The S-Bahn line starts at Wannsee and passes via Zoo, Alexanderplatz and Ostkreuz to Erkner.

Villa in Köpenick

Köpenick is far and away the largest and leafiest suburb in Berlin. The Müggelsee, Langer See, Seddinsee, Zeuthener See and Grosse Krame lakes are all within its boundary. Like the people of Spandau (*see page 53*), the 130,000 residents of Köpenick are proud of their individuality. Both places are notably older than Berlin and are still unhappy about having been incorporated into the capital in 1920.

View across the Dahme towards Kietz

Köpenick's old town is on the island formed by the Spree and the Dahme and can be reached from S-Bahnhof Köpenick via Bahnhofstrasse. Next to the Laurentiuskirche (1841), with its tall brick gable, is the Rathaus (town hall) in the Alt-Köpenick-Strasse, a neo-Gothic brick building dating from 1904.

The whole of Europe was once amused by the tale of the 'Captain of Köpenick'. On 16 October 1906, a shoemaker by the name of Wilhelm Voigt 'arrested' the mayor and disappeared with the town finances. He had 'borrowed' the uniform of a Prussian captain from a junk shop and marched on the town hall with an escort of soldiers whom he had picked up off the streets. Voigt was soon caught but the story was often quoted abroad as a striking example of the Prussian propensity to follow without question anyone in uniform. The full story is told by Carl Zuckmayer in his play of the same name, which premiered in Berlin in 1931.

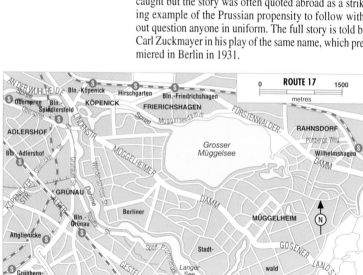

Schloss Köpenick

Between Gartenstrasse and Kietzstrasse stand a number of fishermen's houses built in the 17th and 18th century. They remind visitors that Köpenick was originally founded in 1209 as a fishing village. The baroque Schloss (part of which is closed for renovations until approximately 2001) on the Schlossinsel houses the ★ **Kunstgewerbe-museum** (Museum of Arts and Crafts, *see also page 25*). On display are European crafts from the end of the Middle Ages to the present day. Notable exhibits include wooden furniture from the Renaissance and baroque periods and the Berlin silver service of King Frederick I (1695–8) weighing 675kg (1,450lb), impressively presented on a long table. The Schloss was constructed between 1677–82 by Rutger von Langerfeldt on the site of Elector Joachim II's hunting lodge. In 1730 the splendid heraldic hall was the scene of a court martial of the man who was later to become Frederick the Great and of his friend Lieutenant Katte. A popular annual festival, the Köpenicker Sommer is held in the Schlosspark.

Kunstgewerbemuseum:
Dutch plates c 1520

To enjoy the excellent view of forest and lakes from the **Müggelturm** on the Kleiner Müggelberg, take the bus from Rathaus Köpenick to the 115-m (350-ft) high Müggelberg (Rübezahl stop). The largest of all the Berlin lakes, the **Grosser Müggelsee** covers an area of 17sq km (6sq miles) with a bathing beach and traditional restaurants and has always been a popular destination for Berliners in search of peace and calm. A particular favourite for children is the park in Wuhlheide with its miniature railway. Rowing regattas are held on the Dahme in the district of Grünau.

Erkner lies just inside the Berlin city boundary and is the terminus of the S-Bahn line from Alexanderplatz. Here in the Villa Lassen lived writer Gerhart Hauptmann. There are some good walks to Woltersdorf along the Flakensee and the Löcknitz.

Potsdam's Old Town Hall

Route 18

Potsdam

With a population of 143,000, Potsdam is, in the words of the German poet Jean Paul, 'Berlin's prettiest suburb'. Since 1990, it has been the capital of the Land (state) of Brandenburg, lying in the heart of the peaceful wooded landscape around the Havel lakes to the southwest of Berlin. In 1993, Potsdam celebrated its 1,000th anniversary, as its first mention as Poztupimi was recorded in 993.

The Prussian kings stamped their identity on the town. In the 18th and early 19th centuries, their designers and architects built palaces and planted gardens which rank amongst the finest in Europe. Frederick the Great commissioned Knobelsdorff, Büring, Manger and Gontard, and William III and William IV's legacy was enhanced by Schinkel, Persius, Stüler and the landscape gardener Lenné. Around 3,000 listed buildings and monuments exist in and around Potsdam, the most impressive being the many baroque town houses.

Potsdam elegance

The Nikolaikirche

The best way to get to Potsdam is by crossing the Glienicker bridge, from where Berliner Strasse leads to the **Alter Markt (Old Market)** and the city centre area, combining new and old, which extends almost to the banks of the Havel. Some of the historic parts of the old town which have been preserved are the baroque town hall dating from 1753 with its gilded statue of Atlas supporting a globe, the adjacent baroque Knobelsdorffhaus (1750), Schinkel's neo-classical style **Nikolaikirche** opposite and Knobelsdorff's obelisk of 1753 showing the portraits of Potsdam's four most important architects: Knobelsdorff, Gontard, Schinkel and Persius. There are other fine restored buildings in the central area but they cannot hide the fact that much has been demolished (including the palace in 1960) to be replaced by bare open spaces.

In 1991, after a break of 46 years, the recast bell from Potsdam's demolished Garrison Church rang out again at its new location on the corner of Dortustrasse and Yorckstrasse. Close to the neo-Gothic Nauener Gate dating from 1755 – the two other city gates are the baroque Brandenburger Gate (1770) and the Jägertor (1773) – lies the **Holländische Viertel (Dutch quarter)**. This part of the old town was built between 1734 and 1741 by Jan Boumann, for Dutch settlers. There are 134 red-brick houses in the four squares. Many of the delapidated buildings have now been restored.

The Dutch Quarter

To the north of the town is the Russian colony known as **Alexandrowka,** where 13 Russian log cabins were constructed in 1826. After many years Russian Orthodox services have resumed in the Alexander Nevski church on Kapellenberg. Between Kapellenberg and Pfingstberg a path leads past the Jewish cemetery where the oldest graves date from 1743.

★★★ Schloss Sanssouci

Schloss Sanssouci: parterre and statue

This summer palace was built in rococo style for Frederick the Great by Knobelsdorff between 1745 and 1747. The 97-m (300-ft) garden front with its 35 huge caryatids and dome with the name Sanssouci inscribed in gold letters is very impressive.

The magnificent rococo ★ **interior** of the palace and the art treasures reflect Frederick's personal taste. The Library, the Small Gallery and the Music Room are of particular merit. It was in 1786 at Sanssouci that the celebrated Prussian king died. Frederick the Great's mausoleum, on the right-hand side of the garden at Schloss Sanssouci, is open to visitors.

The eastern side of the splendid ★★ **Schlosspark** grounds were laid out by Knobelsdorff in the style of a French parterre – an ornamental basin surrounded by white marble statues. The western section was designed in the English-Chinese style when the ★ Neues Palais was under construction between 1763 and 1769, following a design by Frederick the Great.

Other buildings in the grounds of Sans Souci are the Picture Galleries, the Chinese teahouse built between 1754–6, the ★ Roman baths designed by Schinkel in 1834 and based on a Roman villa, and the New Orangery which was built by Persius and Stüler in 1850. The ★ **Charlottenhof** classical palace was designed by Schinkel in 1826 for Crown Prince Frederick William.

Chinese teahouse

In 1945, the Potsdam Agreement was signed at ★ Schloss Cecilienhof in the Neues Garten. The original conference room with the round table, as well as the studies of Stalin, Churchill and Trumann, can be visited.

Schloss Cecilienhof: courtyard

Art History

Opposite: in the garden of Schloss Sanssouci: the New Palace

Romanesque and Gothic
The few buildings which survived the Middle Ages have either been substantially altered or were destroyed in World War II. As well as the 13th-century Heiliggeist-kapelle (*see page 27*), the simple, 15th-century Gothic Marienkirche is also of interest. It contains an important late-medieval fresco, the 22-m (70-ft) *Totentanz* (Dance of Death). The restored Nikolaikirche in Spandau also dates from the 15th century.

Spandau's Nikolaikirche

Renaissance
The most significant work from the Renaissance was the Stadtschloss. This palace, built in 1538 by Caspar Theyss for the Prussian kings, stood on the Spreeinsel in the eastern part of Berlin, but it was demolished in 1950-1. Most of the splendid townhouses from that time have also gone, with the exception of a 17th-century house in Breite Strasse occupied by the Ribbeck family who featured in the novels of the local author Theodor Fontane.

79

Baroque
The great architect and sculptor Andreas Schlüter (1664–1718) had a tremendous influence on Berlin's artistic life during the baroque period. One of the most important sculptures of that time is his statue of the *Great Elector on Horseback* which now stands in front of Schloss Charlottenburg. His influence was also to be seen in the extension to the Stadtschloss and in the construction of the armoury in Unter den Linden (1695–1706). Apart from Schlüter, the Swedish architect Eosander von Göthe (1670–1729) and Johann Arnold Nering (1659–95) were responsible for building Schloss Charlottenburg. The churches which were built around 1700 were either destroyed or badly damaged in the last war, eg, the Parochial-kirche, the German Cathedral and the French Cathedral.

Rococo
As soon as Frederick the Great came to the throne in 1740 the rococo style of architecture became popular. Georg Wenzeslaus von Knobelsdorff (1699–1753) was one of its leading proponents. He built the Opernhaus (Opera House) in Unter den Linden, Schloss Sanssouci in Potsdam, redesigned the Potsdamer Stadtschloss and extended the east wing of Schloss Charlottenburg with its Goldene Galerie, a masterpiece of Prussian rococo.

Schloss Charlottenburg: Belvedere Teahouse

Frederick the Great invited many French artists to Berlin, one of whom was the painter Charles Amédée Vanloo. His court painter Antoine Pesne (1683–1757) had worked for Frederick I. One artist who earned himself a

The Brandenburg Gate

Alte Bibliothek, Unter den Linden

*Commemorative temple
to Queen Luise*

reputation for realistic portrayals of his times was the painter and copper engraver Daniel Chodowiecki (1726–1801) from the Baltic port of Gdansk.

The Classical and Romantic period

Classical art and architecture predominated in Berlin from the middle of the 18th century and there are many fine examples still on view. Nothing defines German classicism better than the Brandenburg Gate which was built by Karl Gotthard Langhans (1733–1808), a leading representative of this style. But it was Karl Friedrich Schinkel (1781–1841) who had a major hand in reshaping the central area of the city. Unter den Linden, Neue Wache, the Schauspielhaus in Gendarmenmarkt and the Altes Museum on Museum Island are just a few examples of his legacy to the city.

Gottfried Schadow (1764–1850) who created the quadriga (chariot and horses) for the Brandenburg Gate, and his pupil Christian Daniel Rauch (1777–1857), were the most distinguished sculptors of this period. One example of Rauch's work can be seen on the tomb of Queen Luise in the mausoleum at Schloss Charlottenburg.

There is no question that landscape painter Karl Blechen (1798–1840) represents the essence of German Romantic painting. The Prussian court painter Franz Krüger (1797–1857), architectural painter Eduard Gärtner (1801–77) and painter Theodor Hosemann (1807–75) have all left works which characterise the Biedermeier period, bringing art closer to ordinary people's lives.

Ludwig Tieck (1773–1853), Friedrich Schlegel (1772–1829), E T A Hoffmann (1776–1822) Adelbert von Chamisso (1771–1838) and Achim von Arnim (1781–1831) are all important names associated with the Romantic movement in literature and, by the end of the 18th century, Berlin had become the focus for their followers.

Historicism

With the growth of Berlin around the middle of the 19th century, architects were able to express themselves freely, but their style harked back to the Renaissance and baroque periods. Ludwig Persius (1803–45), Friedrich August Stüler (1800–65) and Johann Heinrich Strack (1805–80), who had been pupils of Schinkel, continued to develop his ideas. Strack built the Nationalgalerie and the Siegessäule (Victory Column). Other buildings from this time are the Rotes Rathaus by H F Waesemann (1813–79), the Reichstag by Paul Wallot (1814–1912) and the Berlin Cathedral by J Raschdorff (1823–1914).

One sculptor who broke fresh ground with his neobaroque style was Reinhold Begas (1831–1911). Adolph von Menzel (1815–1905) glorified the age of Frederick the Great. He epitomised the Berlin school of painting towards the end of the 19th century, but he also painted in a more contemporary style, eg *Das Eisenwalzwerk (The Rolling Mill)* in the Old National Gallery.

The critical approach to realism which was so typical of the Berlin style was also apparent in the writings of Willibald Alexis (1798–1876), Adolf Glassbrenner (1810--76) and Theodor Fontane (1819–98) in particular.

20th century

After 1900, many of the new buildings were functional, eg, warehouses and factories, but the Haus des Rundfunks by Hans Poelzig (1869–1936) and the Olympic Stadium by Werner March (1894–1976) are of interest.

Olympic Stadium, exit to terraces

The heyday of the Berlin painting school was around 1900. The masters of German Impressionism lived and worked there: painter and graphic artist Max Liebermann (1847–1935), portrait artist Lovis Corinth (1858–1925) and the illustrator Max Slevogt (1868–1932). Käthe Kollwitz (1867–1945) and Heinrich Zille (1858–1929) are best known for their socio-critical drawings which portray the poverty of Berlin's working classes.

81

The Expressionists, like the Impressionists, came together in Berlin around 1910 and set in train a movement which spread across Europe. The Berlin Expressionists included Emil Nolde (1867–1956), Max Pechstein (1881–1955), Karl Schmidt-Rottluff (1884–1976), Karl Hofer (1878–1955), Erich Heckel (1883–1969), Max Beckmann (1884–1950) and George Grosz (1893–1959).

Max Pechstein: Bow and Arrow

Hugo Lederer (1871–1938), August Gaul (1869–1921), Georg Kolbe (1877–1947) worked as sculptors. Renée Sintenis created the 'Berlin Bear'.

There are many hundreds of young painters and sculptors of recent generations who have also made their mark beyond the confines of Berlin's artistic circles. A large number of foreign artists have lived and worked in the city, often as a result of an invitation from the Academic Exchange Bureau. At the beginning of the 1980s, the so-called *Junge Wilde* (young wild ones) made a name for themselves and enlivened the artistic scene, but there is no evidence of any uniform trend. Nothing would provide a better insight into the contemporary world of art than a tour round Berlin's many and varied galleries. At one end of the spectrum, the Avantgarde Galerie specialises in 1920s avant garde Russian art and contemporary Russian and German artists, while the Galerie Zwinger encourages original, young and working Berlin artists.

One of the focal points for readers and writers is the Literaturhaus Berlin (Fasanenstrasse 23), a late 19th-century townhouse, which not only hosts events and exhibitions, but also offers a restaurant and a bookshop.

The Berlin Museum

Museums and Galleries

The Man with the Golden Helmet can be seen at the Painting Gallery

Allied Museum, Zehlendorf, Clayallee 135. Tuesday to Saturday 10am–6pm, Wednesday 10am–8pm.

Bauhaus Archive, Museum für Gestaltung (Design Museum), Klingelhöferstr. 14. Monday, Wednesday to Sunday 10am–5pm.

Berggruen Collection Charlottenberg, Spandauer Damm/Schlossstr., Charlottenburg. Tuesday to Friday 9am–5pm, Saturday to Sunday 10am–5pm.

Brecht-Waigel-Gedenkstätte, Mitte, Chausseestr. 125. Brecht's home and study. Forum for literature; bookshop and restaurant. Tuesday to Friday 10–noon, Thursday 5–7pm, Saturday 9.30–noon, 12.30–2pm.

Botanisches Museum, Dahlem, Königin-Luise-Str. 6–8. Tuesday to Sunday 10am–5pm.

Bröhan Museum, Charlottenburg, Schlossstr. 1a. Tuesday to Sunday 10am–6pm.

Brücke Museum, Dahlem, Bussardsteig 9. Daily except Tuesday, 11am–5pm.

Dahlem Museums, Dahlem, Arnimallee 23–27 and Lansstr. 8. Closed for renovation until 2001.

Deutsches Historisches Museum (German Historical Museum) housed in the former armoury at Unter den Linden 2. Closed for renovation until the beginning of 2002.

Georg Kolbe Museum, Charlottenburg, Sensburger Allee 25. Daily except Monday, 10am–5pm.

Gipsformerei (National Plaster Casting Company), Charlottenburg, Sophie-Charlotten-Str. 17–18. Monday to Friday 9am–4pm, Wednesday 9am–6pm. Replicas of well-known statues and busts on view in museums all over the world to purchase.

Hamburger Bahnhof, Mitte, Invalidenstr. 50–51, Tuesday to Friday 9am–5pm, Saturday to Sunday 10am–5pm. Contemporary art by names such as Warhol, Judd and Lichtenstein.

Hugenottenmuseum, Gendarmenmarkt, Mitte, Tuesday to Saturday noon–5pm, Sunday 11am–5pm.

Jewish Museum, Kreuzberg, Lindenstr. 9–14. Tel: 259933 or 2839744 for a guided tour.

Käthe Kollwitz Museum, Fasanenstr. 24. Daily except Tuesday, 11am–6pm.

Kunstgewerbemuseum (Museum of Arts and Crafts), Matthäi-Kirdstrasse 10. Tuesday to Friday 9am–5pm, Saturday and Sunday 10am–5pm.

Kunstgewerbemuseum (Museum of Arts and Crafts), Schloss Köpenick, Schlossinsee. Wednesday to Sunday 10am–6pm.

Märkisches Museum, am Köllnischen Park 5. Wednesday to Sunday 10am–6pm.

Bes Vase, Museum im Schloss Charlottenburg

Martin-Gropius-Bau, Stresemannstr. 110. (Changing exhibitions). Tuesday to Sunday 10am–8pm.

Museum im Schloss Charlottenburg, Luisenplatz 1 and Schlossstr. 70. **Historical Rooms** in the palace, Tuesday to Friday 9am–5pm, Saturday and Sunday 10am–5pm.

83

Deutsche Technikmuseum Berlin (German Museum of Technology Berlin), Kreuzberg, Trebbiner Str. 9. Tuesday to Friday 9am–5.30pm, Saturday and Sunday 10am–6pm.

Museum für Volkskunde (German Folklore), Dahlem, Im Winkel 6. Tuesday to Friday 9am–5pm, Saturday and Sunday 10am–5pm.

Museumsinsel. All museums are open Tuesday to Sunday 9am–5pm.

Musikinstrumentenmuseum (Museum of Musical Instruments), Tiergarten, Tiergartenstr. 1. Tuesday to Friday 9am–5pm, Saturday and Sunday 10am–5pm.

Neue Nationalgalerie, Tiergarten, Potsdamer Str. 50. Tuesday to Friday 9am–5pm, Saturday and Sunday 10am–5pm.

Museum für Naturkunde (Museum of Natural History), Mitte, Invalidenstr. 43. Tuesday to Sunday 9.30am–5pm. Principal attractions here include dinosaur skeletons and the world-famous fossil imprint of an archaeopteryx (prehistoric bird), of which there is a copy in London's Natural History Museum.

Neue Nationalgalerie

Painting Gallery, Matthäi Kirchplatz 4, Tiergarten. Tuesday to Friday 9am–5pm, Saturday and Sunday 10am–5pm.

Schinkelmuseum, in the Friedrichwerdersche church, Werderscher Markt, Mitte. Sculptures from the classical period, the achievements of Schinkel in Berlin. Wednesday to Sunday 10am–6pm.

Music, Theatre and Festivals

The Berlin Philharmonic Orchestra enjoys a worldwide reputation. Berlin can offer theatre-goers a full range of top-class professional productions. Performances under the directorship of Peter Stein at the Schaubühne received critical acclaim throughout Germany. Although Stein is no longer at the Schaubühne, the actor-team of Jutta Laupe, Otto Sander, Bruno Glanz and Edith Clever is described as leading the 'most significant German-speaking company'. There is also a theatre for children, the Grips Theater.

The best way to discover what is going on in Berlin at any given moment is to take a look in one of the three city magazines, *Ticket*, *Tip* or *Zitty*. You'll find current events and performances listed under the the the various headings. Information, tickets, books, posters and brochures for various festival events and performances are available at **Berlin Tourismus Marketing**, am Karlsbad 11, Tiergarten. Tel: 250025, fax: 25002424, Monday to Friday 8am–8pm, Saturday to Sunday 9am–6pm.

Theater des Westens

Opera, Operetta, Musicals

Deutsche Oper Berlin, Bismarckstr. 34–7. Opera, ballet.

Staatsoper Berlin, Unter den Linden 7. Opera and ballet; chamber concerts in the Apollo-Saal.

Komische Oper, Behrenstr. 55–7. Opera, operetta, musicals, ballet.

Schiller Theater, Bismarckstr. 110, Charlottenburg. International musical productions.

Theater des Westens, Kantstr. 12. Musical, operetta.

Concert Halls

Philharmonie and **Kammermusiksaal** (Chamber Music Hall), Kemperplatz. Home of the Berlin Philharmonic.

Grosser Sendesaal des SFB, Masurenallee 8. Concert hall of the Berlin radio symphony orchestra.

Konzerthaus Berlin, Gendarmenmarkt. Concerts, chamber music.

Konzertsaal der Hochschule der Künste, Hardenbergstr. 33.

Theatres

Berliner Ensemble, Bertolt-Brecht-Platz. Brecht and contemporary plays.

Carousel Theater an der Parkaue, Lichtenberg, Hans-Rodenberg-Platz 1. Children's and youth theatre.

Deutsches Theater, Schumannstr. 13a. Classical drama and contemporary productions.

Friedrichstadtpalast, Friedrichstr. 107 (1,900 seats; small revue theatre, 240 seats). Variety.

Friends of Italian Opera, Fidicinstr. 40, Kreuzberg.

Theatre advertising

Small private theatre. English-speaking plays by British and American directors and actors.

Grips Theater, Altonaer Str. 22. The famous children's and youth theatre.

Hansa Theater, Alt-Moabit 47. People's theatre.

Hebbel Theater, Stresemannstr. 29. Plays; many guest performances.

Kammerspiele, Schumannstrasse 13a. Mainly contemporary dramas.

Kleines Theater, Südwestkorso 64. Literary venue.

Komödie, Kurfürstendamm 206. Light entertainment.

Maxim Gorki Theater and **Maxim Gorki Studiobühne,** Am Festungsgraben 2. Modern playwrights.

Renaissance-Theater, Hardenbergstr. 6. Period drama.

Schaubühne am Lehniner Platz, Kurfürstendamm 153. Conventional and experimental drama (three performances at the same time with high-tech stage production). Studio in Cuvrystrasse, Kreuzberg.

Schlosspark Theater, Schlossstr. 48. Primarily modern plays.

Theater am Kurfürstendamm, Kurfürstendamm 206. Popular drama.

Theater unterm Dach, Prenzlauer Berg, Eberswalder Strasse 101. Modern works.

Tribüne, Otto-Suhr-Allee 18–20. Drama, comedy.

UFA-Fabrik, Tempelhof, Viktoriastrasse 10–18. Revues, cabaret, etc.

Vagantenbühne, Kantstr. 12a. Modern and problem dramas.

Volksbühne, Rosa-Luxemburg-Platz. Popular classical and modern theatre.

Wintergarten Varieté, Potsdamer Strasse 96, Tiergarten. Variety shows by André Heller.

Maxim Gorki Theater

85

Cabaret

Die Stachelschweine, Europa Center; **Die Wühlmäuse,** Nürnberger Str. 33; **Klimperkasten,** Otto-Suhr-Allee 100; **Die Distel,** Friedrichstr. 101; **Kartoon,** Französische Strasse 24.

Festivals

Berlin's round of festivals begins with the International Film Festival in February and continues with the *Theatertreffen* in May (10 important German language theatre productions are performed). In July are the *Bachtage* (Bach Days) followed by the *Sommerfestspiele* in July and August, as well as the highly regarded *Berliner Jazztage* in November. The musical events, theatre, film and visual arts during the *Berliner Festwochen* in September attract a lot of interest. Since 1988, the European Film Prize has been awarded in Berlin.

Schultheiss

BIERSTUBE

Öffnungszeiten

Mo-Do   12:00-2

Fr.u.Sa   12:00-2

So   10:00-2

Auf die Schnelle
.. Mikrowelle

Komplett-Menü

Food and Drink

Opposite: no shortage
of sustenance

Berlin specialities

The best traditional Berlin dishes are designed for those
with healthy appetites. Meat dishes predominate with an
overall preference for pork, and particularly *Eisbein*
(knuckle of pork) accompanied by sauerkraut and pease
pudding, or *Kasseler Rippenspeer* (pickled ribs of pork).
Another popular dish is the *Berliner Schlachteplatte* which
consists of fresh blood and liver sausage, pig's kidney and
fresh-boiled pork. *Löffelerbsen Berliner Art* is a thick,
warming soup made from peas with pickled pig's ears,
trotters and tails added.

There are a wide range of local sausages worth trying:
*Bockwurst mit Kartoffelsalat, Jagdwurst, Bierwurst,
Bratwurst* and *Currywurst. Buletten* (meatballs) or
Hackepeter, raw minced beef and pork with onions, are
popular Berlin snacks. *Berliner Pfannkuchen* (Berlin pan-
cakes) are known as 'Berliners' throughout the rest of Germany and resemble doughnuts.

*No German city has a wider
choice of pubs and bars*

87

Beer is always at the top of the drinks order, Schultheiss
Engelhardt and Berliner Kindl being the biggest of Berlin's
breweries. To quench your thirst on hot days, try a *Weisse
mit Schuss* (shots of raspberry or woodruff extract are
added to a glass of light beer).

The less adventurous would probably just have a
straightforward Bavarian pils. *Bock* (strong bottom-
fermented beers), *Korn* (rye whisky) and *Kümmel* (a
liqueur containing caraway seeds, cumin and fennel) are
popular alternatives.

Where to go

A touch of Paris

There are more than 8,000 restaurants, bars, cafés, pubs
(some with live music), breakfast bars, tourist cafés and
beer gardens for weekend excursions, some 1,400 of which
are in the eastern half of the city – no German city has a
wider choice.

Street corner pubs are known as *Kneipen* and are
straightforward beer and drinks bars, which usually do not
serve food. Typical Berlin *Kneipen* are found in
Schöneberg – especially the original Berlin *Destille*
(brandy shop) **Heinz Doll,** Damascekestrasse 26, Charlottenburg, Kreuzberg, as well as Moabit, Wedding,
Prenzlauer Berg and Mitte.

In the west of the city, the list of top-class restaurants
is headed by **Rockendorfs Restaurant** situated in the
north of Berlin (Waidmannslust, Düsterhauptstr. 1) and
Maxwell, Bergstrasse 22, in Mitte – both offer a wide and
interesting range of gourmet food of the highest quality.
Some other eating places with excellent reputations are
Anna e Bruno in Charlottenburg, **Du Pont** in Budapester

Strasse, **Bamberger Reiter** in Regensburger Strasse as well as the restaurants in the international hotels.

The restaurants and bars (Harry's New York Bar, for example) at the Hotel Esplanade on Lützowufer 15 are currently very fashionable. There are no licensing hours or restrictions on opening times in western Berlin, so dining out rarely means starting before 8pm and more often than not its nearer 10pm.

Although most restaurants and *Kneipen* are not open 24 hours a day, many stay open until 2am and some do not close until 4 or 5am. But at about this time of the morning, the *Frühstückskneipen* or breakfast bars are opening. Early birds can start the day with generous portions of breakfast and these bars usually carry on serving only until about 3pm.

As far as ethnic cuisine is concerned, there is hardly a country or region that is not represented in Berlin. Turkish, Greek, Italian and Balkan restaurants abound, but Berlin also has its fair share of Chinese and Indian restaurants, as well as Russian, Danish, French, Polish and many more. Excellent kosher food can be enjoyed at the restaurant in the **Oren** in Oranienburger Strasse.

In the east of the city, there are still relatively few restaurants. They are to be found mostly in the Nikolaiviertel, near Alexanderplatz, in Friedrichstrasse, Oranienburger Strasse, on Gendarmenmarkt and Kollwitzplatz. The only gastronomic high spot in this part of Berlin is the **Forellenquintett** in the Grand Hotel. A very pleasant atmosphere exists at the **Kellerrestaurant im Brecht-Haus** (Chausseestr. 125), where the menu has a distinctly Austrian flavour with recipes by Helene Weigel.

Elegant Kurfürstendamm

Restaurants in the Kurfürstendamm area

International cuisine

Alt-Berliner Schneckenhaus, Viktoria-Luise-Platz; **Alt-Luxemburg**, Windscheidstr. 31; **Bamberger Reiter**, Regensburger Str. 7; **Chalet Corniche**, Königsallee; **Conti-Fischhstuben**, at the Ambassador Hotel; **Du Pont**, Budapester Str. 1; **Florian, Girolmanstr. 52; Frühsammers Restaurant an der Rehwiese**, Nikolassee, Matterhornstr. 101; **Hasenburg**, Kreuzberg, Fichtenstr. 1; **Restaurant im Logenhaus**, Emser Str. 12; **Rockendorfs**, Waidmannslust, Düsterhauptstr. 1.

Florian

Traditional German and Berlin restaurants

Film-Bühne, Hardenbergstr.; **Friesenhof**, Uhlandstr. 185; **Gasthaus Landauer**, Landauer Str. 8; **Hardtke**, Meinekestr. 27 and Grunewald, Hubertusallee 48; **Hecker's Deele**, Grolmanstr. 35; **Heinz Holl**, Damaschkestr. 26; **Luttes und Wagner**, Charlottenstrasse 56,

Mitte; **Mommsen-Eck**, Mommsenstr. 45; **Schultheiss**, at the junction of Kurfürstendamm and Meinekestrasse; **Spree-Athen**, Leibnizstr. 60; **Storch**, Schöneberg. Wartburgstr. 54; **Tafelrunde** (you will find medieval-style dining offered here), Wilmersdorf, Nachodstr. 21.

Restaurants in Berlin-Mitte – Prenzlauer Berg

Borchardt, Französische Str. 47; **Ephraim-Palais**, am Mühlendamm; **Französischer Hof**, am Gendarmenmarkt; **Grand Hotel**, Friedrichstr. 158; **Kellerrestaurant im Brecht-Haus**, Chausseestr. 125; **Offenbach Stuben**, Stubbenkammerstr. 8; **Oren**, Oranienburger Str.; **Reinhard's**, Poststr. 28; **Ribbeck-Keller**, Breite Str. 35; **Sophieneck**, Sophienstr. 37; **Zum Nussbaum**, Am Nussbaum; **Zur letzten Instanz**, Waisenstr. 14 (historic Berlin tavern); **Zur Rippe**, Poststr. 17.

Ausflugslokale (country cafés)

No Berliner's weekend is complete without going for a walk in the woods and stopping for a drink at one of the many local cafés or inns:

Blockhaus Nikolskoe, Wannsee; **Café Liebig**, Grünau, Regattastr; **Eierschale Zenner**, Treptow, Alt-Treptow 14; **Forsthaus Paulsborn**, by the Grunewaldsee; **Grunewaldturm**, Havelchaussee; **Historische Gaststätte Zitadellenschänke**, Spandau, Am Juliusturm; **Lindwerder** on Lindwerder island, Havelchaussee; **Müggelseeperle** by the Grosser Müggelsee; **Morlake**, Morlakenweg 1, am Wannsee; **Neu-Helgoland** by the Kleiner Müggelsee; **Rübezahl** by the Grosser Müggelsee; **Seepavillon Tegel**, Tegelort; **Schildhorn**, Am Schildhorn 4; **Teufelsee** in the Müggelbergen; **Toulouse**, Forsthaus Tegel by the Tegeler See; **Wannsee-Terrassen** by the beach.

Blockhaus Nikolskoe at Wannsee

89

Cafés in the Kurfürstendamm area

Bristol, Kurfürstendamm 35; **Kempinski**, Kurfürstendamm 27; **Kranzler**, Kurfürstendamm 18/19; **Leysieffer**, Kurfürstendamm 218; **Möhring**, Kurfürstendamm 234 (junction of Kurfürstendamm and Uhlandstr); **Monte Video**, Motzstr. 54; **Mövenpick**, Europa Center; **Tasty**, Kurfürstendamm 53; **Wintergarten**, Fasanenstr. 23.

Café Kranzler on the Ku'damm

Cafés in Berlin-Mitte – Prenzlauer Berg

Arkade, Französische Str. 25; **Beth Café**, Tucholskystr. 40; **Café Clara**, Clara-Zetkin-Str. 90; **Café Spreeblick**, Propstr. 9; **Hackbath's**, Auguststr. 49; **Kaffeestube**, Husemannstr. 6; **Krähe**, Kollwitzstr. 84; **Opernpalais**, Unter den Linden 5; **Pressecafé**, Karl-Liebknecht-Strasse; **Tadschikische Teestube**, Palais am Festungsgraben 1; **Telecafé**, the television tower.

Shopping

The main shopping area for west Berlin is around the Kurfürstendamm, leading into Tauentzienstrasse, an extension of the Ku'damm. Situated at the far end of Tauentzienstrasse is one of the biggest department stores in the world, the **Kaufhaus des Westens** or **KaDeWe** as it's better known. On seven floors, with a mini-mall on the ground floor, the store offers an enormous selection of fashions, home furnishings and international specialities, not to mention its unbeatable food hall. Heading back towards the Ku'damm, the **Europa Center**, a shopping mall with more than 100 shops spread over three floors, dominates the area. Nearby is the 'Mini-City', which will interest teenagers. Other city-centre shopping areas are the **Ku'damm-Eck** and the **Ku'damm-Karree**, as well as the new and exclusive **Uhlandpassage**.

Down the side streets in the Ku'damm area, shoppers will find all sorts of interesting and unusual shops. Some are classy and expensive, others are simply bizarre. Then in Fasanenstrasse, Bleibtreustrasse, Schlüterstrasse, Giesebrechtstrasse and Pestalozzistrasse there are shops selling antiques and furniture, along with art galleries and second-hand shops.

Fasanenstrasse antique shop

The Ku'damm is renowned for its book shops, but seek out the **KPM porcelain** showroom and the branch of the **Meissen pottery shop**, the main branch of which is in Unter den Linden. In and around the Ku'damm area there are about 1,100 shops, plus 100 cafés and restaurants. Of the 250 art galleries in Berlin, most are located in this part of the city.

Near Wittenbergplatz in Keithstrasse, Eisenacher Strasse and Motzstrasse and on Viktoria-Luise-Platz the discerning shopper will find the best quality antiques and antiquarian shops, but there are also some interesting junk shops. Every year around the end of November and the beginning of December an important antiques fair known as the '**Antiqua Berlin**' is held. But bargain hunters should also seek out the **Trödelmärkte** (flea markets) dotted around the city. The best-known is the one by Strasse des 17. Juni. Bergmannstrasse in Kreuzberg, around Flughafenstrasse in Neukölln, Winterfeldt- and Eisenacher Strasse in Schöneberg and Schönhauser Allee in Prenzlauer Berg are also areas where flea markets flourish.

Seek out the flea markets

Apart from the city centre, every district has a main shopping street. In Steglitz it is Schlossstrasse, in Charlottenburg it is Wilmersdorfer- and Kantstrasse, in Neukölln the Karl-Marx-Strasse, in Friedrichshagen it's Bölschestrasse and in Weissensee Berliner Allee.

Nightlife

Berliners never seem to take a rest. From late evening to the early hours of the morning Berlin vibrates, offering an enormous choice of bars, nightclubs and discos.

Live music bars

At the weekends, top groups and folk singers perform in the Berlin *Musikkneipen*. Popular venues include:

Café EinStein (literary café) and daad-Galerie (Viennese atmosphere), Kurfürstenstr. 58; Eierschale, Podbielskiallee 50 (in the Landhaus, Dahlem) and Rankestr. 1; Go In (international folk music), Bleibtreustr. 17; Hardrock Café, Meineckestr.; Nashville, Breitenbachplatz 8; Quasimodo (international jazz), Kantstr. 12a; Sophienclub, Mitte, Sophienstr. 6.

Bars, night clubs, discotheques

(*recommended for older guests)
Annabell's*, Fasanenstr. 64; Big Apple, Bundesallee 13/14; Big Eden, Kurfürstendamm 202; Chez nous* (transvestite show), Marburger Str. 14; Dollywood* (transvestite show), Kurfürstenstr. 114–16, in the Sylter Hof; Dschungel, Nürnberger Str. 35; Galerie Bremer*, Fasanenstr. 37; First, Joachimstaler Str. 26; I-Punkt*, Europa Center; Friedrichstadtpalast*, Friedrichstr. 107, Mitte (revues; the girls have the longest legs in Berlin); Jansen (Cocktail bar), Gotenstr. 71, Schlöneberg; La Vie en Rose* (revues), Europa Center; Jansen, Gotenstr. 71, Schöneberg. Cocktail bar. Metropol (3 discos and 8 bars), Nollendorfplatz 5; New Eden*, Kurfürstendamm 71; Tacheles, Oranienburgerstr. 52; Tränenpalast, in the old departure hall at Friedrichstr. S-Bahn station.

Champagne and cocktails

A passing invitation

91

Late night line-up at Friedrichstadtpalast

FRIEDRICHSTADT PA
BERLIN

Getting There

Opposite: journey's end

By plane

Take a taxi from the airport

Berlin has three airports, more than any other German city. Even this is not considered sufficient, however, and the authorities are debating whether to build a new one outside the city boundary in the south. Tegel, on the northwestern edge of the city, is the biggest and newest of Berlin's airports, and it is here that most international flights arrive, including those from London, Paris, Athens, Atlanta, New York, San Francisco and Toronto. From the UK, the principal carriers include British Airways, Lufthansa and United Airlines; flights last about 1½ hours.

Schönefeld, in the southeast corner of the city, is Berlin's second airport and the port of entry for flights from Frankfurt am Main, Hamburg, Vienna, the Balkans, and the Middle and Far East. It's also taking flights from some North American cities, to lighten the ever-increasing load on Tegel.

Tempelhof, close to the city centre, is the airport for domestic flights, but there are links to other European cities including London City Airport.

A regular bus service runs between Tegel and Schönefeld with stops at several strategic points in the city centre. There is an underground station at Tempelhof which gives access to almost anywhere in the city (*see Underground map, back flap*).

93

By train

For visitors from the UK, the best train connections to Berlin are from Ostend in Belgium and The Hook of Holland in the Netherlands. Daily trains leave in the evening to arrive in Berlin early the following morning. Alternatively, take the Eurostar to Brussels and a sleeper to Berlin from there. Zoo station and the Berlin Hauptbahnhof (formerly the Ostbahnhof) are the main arrival and departure points, but trains also stop at the suburban stations of Berlin-Wannsee or Berlin-Spandau. The urban overground train service (S-Bahn) also links Spandau, Staaken, Dallgow, Wustermark, Bredow and Nauen with Charlottenburg (18 trains per day). Every hour there is an S-Bahn train from Wannsee to Potsdam main station, which stops at Griebnitzsee and Babelsberg.

New arrivals at Zoo station

By sea

As well as the ferry connections to the Dutch and Belgian ports described above, there are also car ferry services to Hamburg and Rotterdam both from the UK (Scandinavian Seaways sailings on the Harwich–Hamburg route) and Scandinavia. The former East German port of Warnemünde caters for sailings from Trelleborg in Sweden.

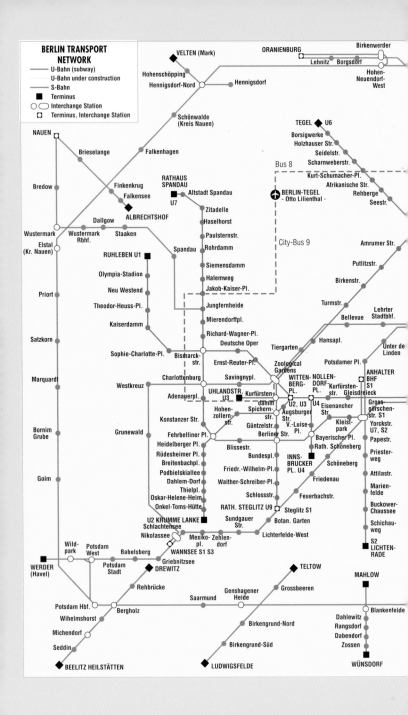

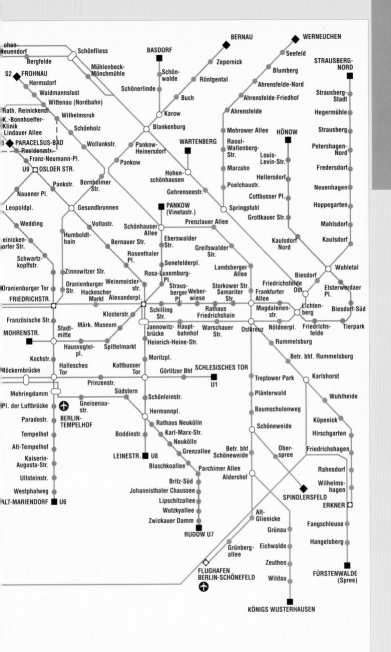

Getting Around

Station attendant

Friedrichstrasse U-Bahn

The Berlin Passenger Transport Executive (BVG) is responsible for the operation of the urban overland S-Bahn and, the undergound U-Bahn, as well as trams and buses. There are **three tariffs**: tariff **A** for a short route passing three stations, tariff **B** which is valid for two hours' travelling by train or bus, and tariff **C** for all trains, buses and trams in the whole area.

Maps of the transport system are free of charge at most underground stations. BVG's customer service offices are located at Potsdamer Strasse 188, Pavillon am Zoo (near the Zoo station) and on Hardenbergplatz. There are similar offices at the S-Bahn stations at Alexanderplatz, Hauptbahnhof, Lichtenberg, Schönefeld, Friedrichstrasse and Schöneweide.

Tariffs

One tariff A ticket for short journeys on the U-Bahn, S-Bahn and buses costs DM 3.90 (children and the unemployed DM 2.60). The fare for tariff B is fixed at DM 3.90, and for tariff C it is DM 4.20. A group of up to five persons can buy a **Gruppenkarte** costing DM 20.00. A **Welcome-Card** costing DM 29.00 can be used for 72 hours and even includes a reduced-entrance charge into some museums, which seems ideal for Berlin visitors.

A *7-Tage-Karte* (seven-day ticket), lasting from Monday to Sunday, is valid for the whole of the network and costs DM 40. All BVG tickets are valid for the whole Berlin network including Potsdam, Schöneiche, Woltersdorf and Strausberg.

U-Bahn (underground)

The Berlin underground (U-Bahn) network with over 100 stations is the most extensive underground system in Germany and it is in the process of being extended. There are a total of nine lines (U1–U9).

At busy periods, the trains run every 2½–5 minutes, with a maximum interval of 10 minutes. They run until 1am and restart at 4am. There is a night bus service marked with an 'N' on the display of the bus, which follows the underground routes. For underground and overland S-Bahn connections *see network map on pages 94–95*.

S-Bahn (suburban railway)

The S-Bahn or Stadtbahn was once one of Berlin's most efficient forms of transport, but it lost much of its importance when the city was partitioned. The stations, many of which were built around the turn of the century, and some of the lines which had been closed down, have now been reopened. Other stations have been turned into markets, galleries, etc. The 10 lines operate almost round the clock between 4am and 2am.

Buses

Buses run every 10 minutes and more frequently during busy periods. There is an all-night service on the main bus routes. The BVG provides a free guide which gives details of the night service. Single and multi-journey tickets can be bought at machines in all underground stations.

Trams

Trams only operate in the east of the city and in the suburb of Potsdam.

There are still trams in Potsdam

Taxis

There are approximately 350 taxi ranks in Berlin and over 100 taxi phones. To call a taxi day and night, tel: Würfelfunk Taxi: 210101; taxi-Ruf im City Funk: 210202; or City Bus (taxis for visitors with large amounts of luggage): 691 6091.

Excursions

BVG coaches run from the Zoo station (Hardenbergplatz) to Schildhorn, the Grunewaldturm, Pfaueninsel (Nikolskoe); from the Wannsee to Pfaueninsel (Nikolskoe); from the Nikolassee S-Bahn station to the beach at Wannsee; from Tegel U-Bahn station to the Tegel beach. These services only run during the summer months and more information can be obtained from the BVG's customer service offices (tel: 19449).

City tours

A number of operators run daily city tours and trips into the countryside. They normally leave from the junction of the Kurfürstendamm and Meineckestrasse or Fasanenstrasse, as well as from the Alexanderplatz by the Forum Hotel Berlin and Friedrichstrasse station (by the IHZ). A full tour round Berlin (3½ hours) will cost DM 39, a shorter tour (2 hours) DM 30. However, a good view of the city for a fraction of the price can be had from the top of a double-decker bus; The number 100 runs from Zoo station through the Brandenburg Gate and on to Alexanderplatz. A tour of the nightclubs (Saturdays only, 4½ hours) costs DM 120 or DM 105 for a shorter tour (3½ hours). Trips to Potsdam leave daily (4 hours) and cost DM 49 or DM 95 for a longer 7-hour trip (3 times a week).

Take a tour bus

Severin und Küln, Kurfürstendamm 216 (tel: 8804 4190) and **Berolina**, Meinekestr. 3 (tel: 88 56 80 30) organise bus tours through the city and to Potsdam.

Canal boat by Museum Island

Stattreisen Berlin, Malplaguestr. 5, Wedding (tel: 455 3028) organise guided walks through different areas of the city.

Kultur Büro Berlin, Greifenhagener Str. 62, Prenzlauer Berg (tel: 444 0936) offers themed city tours such as Berlin from 1933 to 1945, the Twenties, Berlin – city of literature – and the Scheunenviertel.

Boat trips

Scheduled year-round ferries ply between Wannsee and Kladow. On the Kiewitt to Hermannswerder, from Wendenschloss to Grünau and from Oberschöneweide, Wilhelmstrand to Baumschulenweg.

During the summer months, there are services between the Glienicker bridge and Sacrow, from Grünau regatta course to the Langer See, from Schmöckwitz to the Grosse Lanke, from Friedrichshagen to the Müggelseeperle, Rübezahl, from Rahnsdorf, Müggelwerderweg to Müggelhort and from Rahnsdorf church to Müggelheim, Spreewiesen.

The helm of the Havel ferry

The Berlin shipping companies offer many more routes which follow the upper and lower Havel and Tegeler See or pass along some of Berlin's canals right through the heart of the city to Tegel or along to the Pfaueninsel. The various shipping companies (eg, Reederei Riedel, Stern- and Kreisschiffahrt, Reederei Winkler) can provide more detailed information to travellers (tel: 803 1055).

In the east of the city, the Weisse Flotte operates some regular services and excursions along the Havel and the Berlin lakes. Most of the company's services start from the jetty near the S-Bahn railway station at Treptow, but they also call in at Köpenick, Neue Mühle, Grünau and Friedrichshagen.

Tegeler See

Facts for the Visitor

Visas
Visas are not required for citizens of European Union countries; a valid identity card or passport are enough to ensure entry and exit. Holders of Australian, Canadian, Japanese, New Zealand, South African and US passports automatically get three-month permits on crossing the border but visas are required for longer stays.

Customs
Non-EU members can bring 400 cigarettes, one bottle of spirits, two of wine and 50g of perfume; EU-members have guide levels of 800 cigarettes, 10 litres of spirit and 90 litres of wine. Customs keep a close watch for illegal drugs.

A nostalgia trip for motorists

Motorists
The former GDR's version of the Highway Code has been replaced by the Federal German traffic regulations. On some stretches of motorway a 100 km/h (60mph) limit has been imposed and it is likely to apply until the road surfaces have improved.

Automobile clubs in west Berlin: ADAC, Bundesallee 29, Wilmersdorf; AvD, Wittenbergplatz 1, Schöneberg.

Tourist information
For information abroad, contact the offices of the German National Tourist Office.

In the UK: German National Tourist Office, Nightingale House, 65 Curzon Street, London W1Y 7PE, tel: 0900 1600100 (automated service).

In the US: German National Tourist Office, 444 South Flower Street, Suite 2230, Los Angeles CA 90071, tel: (213) 688 7332, fax: (213) 688 7574; Chanin Building, 122 East 42nd Street, 52nd floor, New York, NY 10168, tel: (212) 6617200.

All local enquiries can be made at the **Berlin Tourismus Marketing**, Am Karlsbad 11, 10785 Berlin-Tiergarten, tel: 250025, fax: 2500 2424, Monday to Friday 8am–8pm, Saturday and Sunday 9am–6pm. In response to demand, the office sends out Berlin Information Packs free of charge. Other tourist offices are in the **Europa Center**, Budapester Strasse, 1st floor, Charlottenburg, Monday to Saturday 8am–8pm, Sunday 9am–9pm; in the **Brandenburger Tor**, South Wing, daily 9.30am–6pm; Tegal Airport, main entrance hall, daily 5am–10.30pm and the **Travel Center** in the KaDeWe, 1st floor, Monday to Friday 8.30am–8pm, Saturday 9am–4pm.

For information about the Berlin festival weeks, the **Infoladen** (Info shop) at the Berliner Festspiele GmbH, Budapester Str. 50, 10787 Berlin-Schöneberg is the best

Late-night shopping is Thursdays

place to turn to. Fortnightly listings of cultural, political and other events appear in *Tip, Zitty,* and *Ticket. Berlin-Programm* comes out monthly along with *Checkpoint* which publishes news and information in English.

Libraries

Every district in Berlin has its own library, but the best collections of books are to be found in the western half of the city and include the Amerika-Gedenk-Bibliothek, Blücherplatz 1, Kreuzberg.

Opening times

Shops in the city are generally open from 10am to 8pm, Some even open on Sunday from 10am to 6pm, especially on Unter den Linden and in the Nikolaiviertel. On Saturday, they close at 4pm.

Currency and exchange

The basic unit of German currency is a mark (DM), divided into 100 pfennigs. Coins come in 1, 2, 5, 10 and 50 pfennig denominations, and 1, 2, and 5 marks; notes start at DM 5.

100

Banks close for lunch

Foreign currency can be changed into German marks at all banks, as well as in large hotels. Banks are usually open from 9am–3pm (Monday and Wednesday until 6pm). There is also no shortage of *Wechselstuben* (bureaux de change). The main exchange counter at Zoo station is open Monday to Saturday 8am–9pm, Sunday 10am–6pm, and the one at Tegel Airport is open Monday to Sunday 8am–10pm. A number of banks, especially on Kurfürstendamm, are also open on Saturdays. There are teller machines everywhere which accept Eurocards and other credit cards.

Shopping for postcards

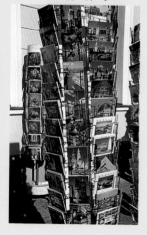

Tipping

Even though service is now officially included everywhere, tipping is still customary and most bills are rounded off.

Public holidays

1 January (New Year); Shrove Tuesday; Good Friday; Easter Monday; 1 May (May Day); Ascension Day; Whit Monday; Corpus Christi; 15 August (The Assumption); 3 October (German Unification Day); 1 November (All Souls' Day); Christmas Day and Boxing Day.

Post offices

There are post offices with long hours at Zoo station (6am–10pm; main poste restante facilities) and at Tegel airport (daily 6.30am–9pm). The post office at Marburger Str. 12 (Monday to Friday 8am–6pm, Saturday 8am–noon) is convenient for the Ku'damm area.

Telephoning

Pay telephones accept 10-pfennig, 50-pfennig, DM 1 and DM 5 coins, or telephone cards. Long-distance telephone calls can be made from the post office, which saves you having to pay the hefty surcharges levied by hotels. For other countries, first dial the international access code 00, then the country code as follows: Australia 61; France 33; Japan 81; Netherlands 31; Spain 34; United Kingdom 44; US and Canada 1. The code for Germany is 49, for Berlin 030. US phone card access numbers include: AT&T 0130 0010; MCI 0130 0012; Sprint 0130 0013.

Public telephone

Time

Germany is six hours ahead of US Eastern Standard Time and one ahead of Greenwich Mean Time.

Medical

Visitors from the EU can claim health services available to Germans. UK visitors should obtain Form E111 from the Department of Health prior to departure, but private health cover is also recommended.

Chemists are open Monday to Saturday noon. The addresses of chemists open at weekends are clearly posted on the doors.

Emergency numbers

Police (Polizei): 110
Ambulance and Fire Brigade (Notarzt und Feuerwehr): 112
Emergency Medical Service (Ärztliche Notdienst): 310031
Emergency Chemist's Service: 1141

Lost property

The address of the Berlin transport network's lost property office is Fundbüro der BVG, Potsdamer Str. 184, Schöneberg, tel: 25623040. For lost property handed to the police, the address of the Fundbüro der Polizei (lost property office) is Tempelhofer Damm 1, Tempelhof, tel: 6995.

Consulates

Australia: Uhlandstr. 181, tel: 8800880.
Canada: Friedrichstr. 95, tel: 2611161 or 203120.
UK: Unter den Linden 32–4, tel: 2018 4158 or 201840.
US: Neustädische Kirchstrasse 4, Mitte, tel: 2385174.

Cultural centres

Amerika-Haus, Hardenbergstr. 21–4, tel: 819 7661.
British Council, Hardenbergstr. 20, tel: 310176.
Maison de France, Kurfürstendamm 211, tel: 8818702.

The Berlin Hilton

Accommodation

Hotels

There are around 37,000 hotel beds in Berlin, with an increasing number of them in the eastern part of the city. The following is a selection ranging from the very expensive to the moderately-priced in the most popular parts of the city.

Kurfürstendamm - Berlin Mitte

$$$$$

Berlin Hilton, Mohrenstr. 30, Gendarmenmarkt; **Bristol Hotel Kempinski**, Kurfürstendamm 27; **Inter-Continental**, Budapester Str. 2; **Maritim Grand Hotel**, Friedrichstrasse 158; **Grand Hotel Esplanade**, Lützowufer 15; **Radisson Plaza Hotel Berlin**, Karl-Liebknecht-Str. 5; **Steigenberger**, Berlin 30, Los-Angeles-Platz 1; **Schlosshotel Vierjahreszeiten**, Brahmsstr. 4–10.

$$$$

Palace

Ambassador, Bayreuther Strasse 42; **Hotel Berlin**, Lützowplatz 17; **Hotel Brandenburger Hof**, Eislebner Strasse 14; **Hotel Metropol**, Friedrichstrasse 150–3; **Mondial**, Kurfürstendamm 47; **Palace**, in the Europa Center; **Penta**, Nürnberger Str. 65; **Savoy**, Fasanenstr. 9–10; **Schweizerhof**, Budapester Strasse 21–31.

$$$

Agon, Xantener Strasse 4; **Alsterhof**, Augsburger Str. 5; **Art Hotel Sorat**, Joachimstaler Strasse 28–9; **Askanischer Hof**, Kurfürstendamm 53; **Astoria**, Fasanenstr. 2; **Avantgarde**, Kurfürstendamm 14–15; **Berlin Mark Hotel**, Meinekestr. 18–19; **Berlin Excelsior**, Berlin 12, Hardenbergstrasse 14; **Berlin Plaza**, Knesebackstr. 63; **Hotel Berolina**, Karl-Marx-Allee 31; **Hotel Bremen**, Berlin 15, Bleibtreustr. 25; **Charlottenhof**, Charlottenstr. 52; **Hotel City**, Kurfürstendamm 173; **Hotel Consul**, Knesebeckstr. 8–9; **Curator Hotel Berlin**, Grolmanstr. 41–43; **Domus**, Uhlandstr. 49; **Forum Hotel Berlin**, Alexanderplatz; **Frauenhotel Artemisia**, Brandenburgische Str.

Am Zoo

18; **Frühling am Zoo**, Kurfürstendamm 17; **Hamburg**, Landgrafenstr. 4; **Hecker's Hotel**, Grolmanstr. 35; **Kurfürstendamm am Adenauerplatz**, Kurfürstendamm 68; **President**, An der Urania 16–18; **Residenz Berlin**, Meinekestr. 9; **Spreehotel**, Wallstr. 59; **Sylter Hof**, Kurfürstendamm 116.

$$

Atlanta, Fasanenstr. 74; **Börse**, Kurfürstendamm 34; **Bogota**, Schlüterstr. 45; **Fischerinsel**, Neue Ross Strasse 11; **Gendarm Garni**, Charlottenstrasse 60; **Savigny**, Brandenburgische Str. 21; **Sachsenhof**, Motzstr. 7;

Pension Iris, Uhlandstr. 33; **Pension Knesebeck**, Knesebeckstr. 86.

Funkturm and Exhibition Centre area
Seehof, Lietzenseeufer 11 ($$$$); **Am Studio**, Kaiserdamm 80–1 ($$$); **An der Oper**, Bismarckstr. 100 ($$$); **Hotel Brandies**, Kaiserdamm 27 ($$$); **Villa Kastania**, Kastanienallee 20 ($$$); **Hotel von Korff**, Kaiserdamm 29 ($$$).

Hotels in Potsdam
Schlosshotel Cecilienhof, Im Neuen Garten ($$$$$); **Hotel Bayerisches Haus**, Im Wildpark 1 ($$$$); **Wohnen im Holländerhaus**, Kurfürstenstr. 15 ($$$); **Hotel am Schwielowsee**, Am Schwielowsee 110, 14542 Werder ($$); **Pension Bürgerstuben**, Jägerstr. 10 ($).

Hotels in a parkland setting
Haus Bismarck, Bismarckallee 3 ($$$); **Müggelsee**, Köpenick, by the Grosser Müggelsee ($$$); **Landhaus Schlachtensee**, Bogotastr. 9 ($$$); **Seehotel Berlin Friedrichshagen**, Müggelseedamm 288–92 ($$$); **Pension Diana**, Wernerstr. 14a ($$); **Forsthaus Paulsborn**, Am Grunewaldsee ($$); **Hotelpension Diana am See**, Königsallee 40 ($$).

Young people
Information about the youth hostels can be obtained from Deutsche Jugendherbergswerk, Tempelhofer Ufer 32, 10963 Berlin-Kreuzberg, tel: 2623024. It is advisable for youth hostellers from overseas to become members of the International Youth Hostel Federation (IYHF). Here is a list of accommodation for young people in Berlin:

Jugendherberge Ernst Reuter, Hermsdorfer Damm 48–50; **Jugendgästehaus Central**, Nikolsburger Str. 2–4; **Jugendgästehaus Berlin**, Kluckstr. 3; **Jugendgästehaus am Wannsee**, Badeweg 1; **Jugendgästehaus am Zoo**, Hardenbergstr. 9a; **Studentenhotel** (student hostel), Meiningerstr. 10.

Campsites
There are three campsites in the west of the city at **Kladow**, **Dreilinden** and **Haselhorst**. They are open all the year round and pitches can be reserved through the Deutscher Camping Club e.V., Geisbergstrasse 11, Schöneberg. The following campsites are located in the east: the Internationaler Campingplatz by the **Krossinsee** (open all the year round) and the sites at **Geltow**, **Caputh**, **Ferch**, **Werder** and **Glindow** (all in the Potsdam area) and **Neuseddin** and **Kleinmachnow** (south of Zehlendorf).

Shooting the breeze

Index